ENTREBUSINESS

Hi Tom,

Thanks so much for letting me be your coach. I look forward to a bright future.

The best is yet to come!

Jared Polk

ENTREBUSINESS

7 Leadership Principles for Entrepreneurial Success

JARED POLAK

LUCIDBOOKS

TABLE OF CONTENTS

INTRODUCTION

"I met in the street a very poor young man who was in love. His hat was old, his coat worn, his cloak was out at the elbows, the water passed through his shoes, and the stars through his soul."

—Victor Hugo, *Les Miserables*

Our world is full of stories. Whether they are paintings discovered on the wall of a cave or a joke told in passing on the way to work, narratives fill every nook and cranny of every culture. Stories are our entertainment, our education, our connection, and the way we see the world. And perhaps no story is quite as strong as the story of a journey.

From Homer's *Odyssey* to L. Frank Baum's *Wizard of Oz* to J.R.R Tolkien's *The Hobbit,* journeys have captivated our imaginations and led us to consider greater themes of rescue and redemption. What is it about these stories that holds our collective attention? Why do we continue to unfold them in our laps like giant roadmaps, losing ourselves in the stories so fully that the character's adventures become our own?

Perhaps it's because on some level, each of our lives is also a journey. If you laid our lives flat and drew a line from birth to death, charting every detour, backtrack, and pit stop along the way, you would have a journey just as rich as Dorothy's trek down the yellow brick road. And the lessons learned would often be even more profound.

My own adventure began when I was starting a career as a beverage salesman. I didn't grow up thinking like an entrepreneur. Instead, I was all about the traditional structure of traditional business. Like Jackson Strong, the main character of this book, my preconceptions were rocked by some key individuals and experiences. I realized that the solid foundation I thought I was standing on had actually engulfed my feet and was holding me in place. With a little help, I broke free and started moving forward. I discovered that wisdom in business isn't just about reading all the bestsellers and retaining what they teach; it's also about living life as a human being and applying what we experience to business. I didn't have the resources or money, but I managed to build up my own business. And I'm still on that journey today—the journey of growing a business while maintaining a balanced life—of shaping the business and life I want to create.

As business coaches, my colleagues and I have the opportunity to join people on their journey. Many have just started the adventure of a new business—branching off on their own—a challenging new path to hike. But a problem that we often encounter as we join entrepreneurs on this new path is that the journey we think we are making is different from the one we see. There are pre-existing narratives about business that are often quite compelling. Many of them entice entrepreneurs with promises of easy work and guaranteed success. They promote a journey whose end goal of wealth overshadows the character traveling the path in the first place. And if we adopt these narratives as our own, they come with a bundle of beliefs and expectations that can weigh us down and distract us from what really matters—voyaging well.

Part of my job is to listen to the experiences, thoughts, fears, and strategies of entrepreneurs and help them navigate the next bend in their adventure. Through the years, I have recognized some common missteps along the way, but I've also learned principles that can breathe life into any business. Think of them as landmarks on your map—ideas that stand out from the landscape to help you orient and navigate.

I've chosen to share what I've learned in the form of a story. Jackson Strong is an everyday entrepreneur—someone who has found a measure of success and believes he has everything it takes to move to the next level. He is any of us at our most vain. But through the course of one day full of inconveniences, Jackson learns that the journey he is on is not just about success—it's about his character in the midst of success.

My hope is that as you join Jackson on his adventure, the principles he learns about life and business leap off the page like signposts. May you see your own journey in a new light and come to view each inconvenience of business as the invitation it can be. After all, as GK Chesterton once wrote, "An adventure is only an inconvenience rightly considered."

CHAPTER 1

Jackson Strong stood outside the restaurant, blowing into his hands and rubbing them together in an effort to halt the chill of the night air. He had forgotten how cold a Houston winter could be. For a moment he wished there were more of a lining to his Brook's Brothers sports coat, but he knew it would probably just look bulky and weird. He wanted his friends and associates to look at him and see the vanguard of new Houston success, not some snow-phobic weakling huddled into a snowmobile jacket. Besides, being cold was the least of his worries at the moment. He didn't have a reservation.

El Presidente Tapas y Vino was the newest restaurant in a series of international dining experiences in downtown Houston. They had been booked solid every night for the last month and a half. When Jackson called to make his reservation, the maître d' actually giggled. But that only made Jackson want it more. It was the perfect place for him to announce the big news to his people.

Jackson glanced at his watch. 5:30. He had thirty minutes to get a table before his employees started showing up ready for the best food and wine Houston had to offer. He closed his eyes and visualized the biggest table in the restaurant—the one secluded in the private back room, which he knew they had. In his mind, he started populating the room with the people he had already invited. It was a trick he had learned from Bill Parsons, an old boss: visualize the win. Underneath all the pretense of reservations and waiting lists, the room was a sale, which was why Jackson knew the table was as good as his. He ratcheted up his grin into a charming smile and reached for the door.

"Jackson!" The voice startled him and broke his concentration. His mental picture of the room started to fade. He didn't need to turn to know who it was. Only one person would show up this early at such an inopportune moment—his business partner Matthew.

"Matthew, welcome," Jackson said. "You're early."

"I just had an appointment with Vince, who's literally right around the corner, so I thought I would come right over. Figured we could chat a bit before everyone gets here."

Jackson gritted his teeth through his smile. Chatting with Matthew always led to a discussion of what they could "do better," especially whenever he met with his business coach, Vince. This night was meant to be a celebration of everything they had already done perfectly; they had the revenue to prove it. Jackson didn't have the time or the energy for a Matthew chat. Besides, not even Matthew knew the big news yet—the secret he'd been developing over the last few months. And Jackson was certain when Matthew found out later that night, he'd be partying with the rest of them, Vince and "doing better" nothing more than a quickly fading memory.

"I'd love to," Jackson said, "but I need to book our room for dinner."

Matthew's mouth hung open, which made Jackson's smile double in size. "You don't have a reservation?"

"I don't need one. The room is as good as mine. This is *our* night." Before Matthew could protest more, Jackson turned and stepped into the restaurant.

* * *

The back room was even more delightful than Jackson had imagined. It was like stepping into a Restoration Hardware catalog, with beautiful rafters, exposed lighting, and a giant wooden table in the center of the room. He could tell Matthew was still sorry for the birthday party that had been moved back out into the main dining area, so Jackson made sure to order him a full bottle of the best wine the sommelier had to offer. He was still buzzing from the win. Thankfully the maître d' had the heart of a businessman who just needed a little extra commission to make everything work.

Jackson looked around the table at his friends, business associates, and a couple key employees. They were happily washing down their exquisite tapas with mouthfuls of vintage wine. He glanced through the menu one more time, taking pleasure from the fact that he had already ordered one of everything for the table.

Jackson realized that to the rest of the diners, his private party had all the markings of a celebration—and it was. His business, MadeStrong Inc., had just brought in their first million dollars of revenue, all thanks to their pilot product: GoCoNutty. Jackson hated the name and had already fired the marketing manager responsible for it. But there was no way to change it now that it had its own niche on the market. It was the fastest-selling coconut water in Texas and was one of only a few Jackson knew of that were pasteurized using High Pressure Processing instead of heat, helping preserve freshness and vitamin content. GoCoNutty had been his partner Matthew's idea, but Jackson was the one who translated it from dream into reality. And now they could afford to celebrate in a way that turned heads.

Jackson tipped back a glass of 2008 Tinta de Toro and smiled to himself. Not even Matthew was privy to what he was going to unveil. Jackson liked having that kind of power—knowing something that would change the dynamic of the evening and it was his choice whether or not to divulge it. The rush of the wine crawled through his veins up to his head. Life was good, and it was all thanks to him.

It was time to drop the big news. Jackson stood up and steadied himself with a hand on the table. He lifted his wine glass, and his guests hushed each other. "Our fearless leader," he overheard someone say, which widened his grin.

"My fellow Americans," he began, eliciting a handful of giggles. "In all seriousness, it is an honor to be able to treat you all to such a superb celebratory dinner. GoCoNutty's success still feels like a dream, and I can't believe that it only took six months to reach our first million. But I didn't just gather you here to bask in the glow of success. I also wanted to share some big news."

Jackson looked around the table, drawing out the suspense. Matthew caught his eye with a raised eyebrow, which is exactly what Jackson wanted. GoCoNutty had never felt fully his because it had started as Matthew's idea. This new venture would be his alone, and all the praise, success, and profit would rightly belong to him.

"As CEO of MadeStrong, it is my duty not to just sit back on my coattails and ride out the life of one product, but to innovate. I've been working with some of the best minds in product development to create our next big game-changer. Our customers deserve a product with the same attention to taste and texture as GoCoNutty, but they need something a bit more suave—a drink they wouldn't be afraid to take to a dinner party at their boss's house. I'm pleased to announce that we have found that product, and it's called . . . Nighthawk."

The room filled with applause. Jackson considered lifting his arms in the air like a victorious gladiator or benevolent king. Then he noticed that Matthew's clapping was a bit slower than the rest.

"Nighthawk is the fresh-tasting, coconut brew nobody knew they wanted. Using the leftover coconut flesh from our plantation in Thailand, we found the perfect way to brew it with both an IPA and a stout, creating a delicious light and dark version of Nighthawk certain to appeal to the Millennials who've made GoCoNutty such a success. I've had the pleasure of taste-testing both, and let me tell you . . . actually I don't really remember much other than waking up the next day with a delightful hangover and fuzzy memories of some PG-13 rated debauchery. So let's just say it works!"

From the midst of the laughter and more applause, Matthew mouthed, "We need to talk." It was annoying and just like Matthew. Jackson almost frowned at the thought of being subjected to more pessimistic hee-hawing, but he caught himself. This was *his* party, and not even Matthew was going to spoil it.

"Everyone raise your glass," Jackson commanded. "It's been a wild ride, and it's about to get crazier. Here's a toast to the future when we hit three million!" Everyone tipped back their wine and cheered.

"This is my jungle," Jackson thought as he sat down. "I'm the king."

* * *

Slowly the room emptied, each guest stopping by Jackson to offer their gratitude and excitement for Nighthawk. The mix of praise and alcohol engulfed him, and he couldn't hide his grin, even when the party dwindled down to just him and Matthew.

Jackson motioned to Matthew's glass, but he just shook his head. With a shrug, Jackson tipped the remaining wine into his own glass.

"Nighthawk?" Matthew finally asked.

"It has a nice ring to it, doesn't it? Like your night is bound to be swift and sleek—like you're on the hunt."

"To me it sounds like something hidden in shadows . . . which it was."

"You feel out of the loop."

"Of course I do! I'm your partner. Do you have any idea how idiotic I felt learning about this alongside our employees?"

"I wanted it to be a surprise!"

"Well, it was. I'm guessing the board has no idea either."

Jackson cringed and didn't try to hide it. The "board" was an informal group of some of Matthew's local business heroes—CEO's and managers with years of experience. And for Jackson, that was the problem. They'd been doing business a particular way for many years and couldn't seem to grasp the changing markets. They were all conservative and couldn't ever grasp what he was trying to do. But it was Jackson who had to deal with them as CEO. Every advisory meeting was like trying to explain the Internet to his grandfather.

"The 'board' doesn't factor in. Not until they understand what we're trying to do."

"So why do we even have them in the first place?"

"You tell me." Jackson regretted the direction of the conversation, but he didn't know how to stop. They were supposed to be celebrating—getting drunk and giving awkward high-fives like the old days. Instead, Matthew wouldn't look him in the eye.

Jackson reached out to give Matthew a friendly punch on the shoulder. "But you have to admit, it's a great idea."

Matthew frowned. "The problem isn't the idea. Kids will go gaga for coconut-flavored, organic anything. I'm worried about timing."

"Timing?" Jackson almost spit out the last of his wine. "Do you *read* our monthly financials, or are they just desk decorations."

"We need to read *and* understand them."

"Are you suggesting I don't understand my own company's financials?"

"No, it's not that. It's just that you're reading the numbers like an optimistic sales guy."

Jackson laughed. "Relax, Matthew. You're being too uptight. We're sitting on top of a gold mine right now, and you're worried about the weather."

Matthew looked around the room before leaning in. "I've been speaking with Vince about some of our current processes. He's helped me put some things in perspective."

"Vince your business coach? As in someone you pay to tell you things you already know?"

"More like someone who's helped me see a new side to everything. I think you should talk to him."

"OK, now you're actually making me angry. I know how to run my business. Did you forget what we were celebrating tonight?"

"The first million in *revenue*. But if you look closely at what it took to get there, we're bleeding money. Between the marketing and shipping logistics of GoCoNutty and the day-to-day costs of operation, we're in the hole. Even with the million we made."

"That's natural. Everyone knows you have to spend money to make money. It'll all even out eventually. Especially when the one million starts growing."

Jackson picked up the wine bottle, but only a thin trickle splashed into his glass. "Sounds like all you've been coached into is some pansy-waist, conservative business philosophy." He felt the sharp sting of regret as soon as he said it, but it was Matthew's fault. He didn't understand. He could never do Jackson's job. He was the empty wine bottle—the party-ender.

"I'm going to leave now," Matthew said as he stood up. "If you want to have a real conversation about this, I'd suggest it happen in the near future." There was the scrape of a chair, a thank-you to their hostess, and then he was gone.

"Or else?" Jackson yelled. But the room was empty. Jackson sat alone among the empty bottles, used napkins, and half-eaten plates. He was the king, but his kingdom was empty.

* * *

The streetlights and glowing signs of downtown Houston bathed everything in amber, almost as if Jackson were stepping into an old photograph of the city. He shielded his eyes against the nearest light and stumbled across the street. There were plenty of taxis, but he couldn't imagine going home in his current state. Being drunk would normally be enough to stop him from hitching the long ride back home to the northern suburbs, but coupled with the toxic conversation with Matthew—he didn't have the mindset or energy to go back to his empty house. He almost found himself wishing for the passive-aggressive, machine-gun questioning of his ex-wife Karen.

Instead, Jackson started making his way toward the corner. The sidewalk flashed with dull red from a neon sign above his head. Gentleman's Sports and Spirits. He could care less about the sports, but spirits sounded promising. In his eagerness to enter, he nearly tripped over a pair of legs extending out onto the sidewalk. The red glow of the sign made it seem as if they were a phantom pair of severed legs splayed out across his path, but then Jackson heard a cough and a shuffle. A shadowy figure was slumped against the wall of the bar. He could just barely make out a tattered, olive green coat with some type of fake fur lining peeking out against the man's dark skin. The man's eyes were white against the shadows, with little flecks of yellow in their corners. He caught Jackson's startled gaze and stared back. Jackson didn't know whether to apologize for tripping over him or berate him for obstructing the sidewalk with his dirty legs. Before he could make up his mind, the man spoke.

"I'm sorry for that. Thought you saw me here. You're walking all over the place."

"You can't just sit across sidewalks like that."

"I was just resting for a moment."

"Well, next time just don't rest in my way." Jackson started to step over him, but the man reached up and touched his arm. "Don't touch me," Jackson said, pulling his arm back in disgust."

"Please. I just need a dollar for a coffee. It's cold." The man kept his hand outstretched, palm up. In the red light they looked worn and smooth, as if they were molded out of plastic.

"If I give you a dollar, it's only going to last as long as that coffee. In fact, I bet it wouldn't even last that long. It's easy for people like you to waste what you didn't earn. Here are three pieces of advice: pull yourself up off that wall, stop getting in the way of people, and find a job."

The man shrunk back into his shadow, his face drooping in disappointment. Jackson gingerly stepped over the man's legs, pushed against the worn wooden door, and entered the bar.

The crowd was a mix of young professionals and middle-agers like Jackson. Everyone had the markings of both success and boundless drinking: heavy-lidded eyes, tailored suits, impeccable shoes, and a cologne of expensive booze. He fit right in.

Sidling up to the bar, Jackson ordered an old-fashioned with a splash of Perucchi Rojo instead of sugar, just to see if the bartender could keep up. The drink was in his hand in two minutes, perfectly blended. He tried to remember the name of the bar to add to his list of downtown favorites but was finding it difficult to follow any train of thought for more than a couple of seconds. He flagged the bartender.

"What's the name of this place?"

"Gentleman's."

"You're pretty good at what you do. I'm going to remember this place."

"Whatever you say, buddy."

"The only downside is the bums hanging around outside."

"They don't really hurt anyone. Some of them are interesting."

"I'm not talking about them hurting *people*. I'm saying they hurt your business. They work against what you do."

The bartender turned his attention to a raised hand at the other end of the bar. "Well," he said as he started moving the other way, "you're the first to complain to me about it. Makes you think."

Jackson pushed off the bar and made a mental note to call the manager and complain about the conversation. Any person who defended homeless loiterers probably shouldn't be in such a public position.

Soon he was floating through the crowd, smiling at all the blurry, pretty people. The drink in his hand seemed to be always full, and everything Matthew had said dried up word by word to make room for more alcohol. Jackson heard himself mention Nighthawk to more than one stranger. He also found he couldn't say the word "GoCoNutty" without breaking down into fits of giggling. The room started spinning, but he felt stationary—the lone anchor in a sea of people who wanted to be like him. He tried to shout but discovered his tongue was stuck in place. His whole body was moving in slow motion, but he felt himself pushing through a door. A shadow flitted across his line of sight, obscuring everything, sucking the light out of all that was around him. Then he passed out.

CHAPTER 2

The first thing Jackson noticed as he regained consciousness was his leg. He was seated, and his right leg was sticking out awkwardly in front of him, his navy blue suit pants patched with mud and grime. He had no memory of where he was. Everything was purely sensation—the cold air on the tip of his nose, the sunlight making him squint, something hard pushing into his back, his head throbbing and pounding like an audition for a heavy metal band. He looked at his leg and tried to piece together what was going on. Then full consciousness crashed back into his body.

He had been meeting new friends at a sports bar when everything went dark. Jackson remembered drinking—a lot—and figured he must have wandered into the street and passed out. Had he been lying there all night?

Jackson frantically pushed himself off the wall he was sitting against and stood up. That's when he realized he was sitting in the same place as the homeless bum from the night before. He looked down and saw that instead of his tailored navy Brooks Brothers sports coat, he was wearing an olive green trench coat lined with fake fur that smelled like gasoline. The bum's coat. He had been robbed.

He patted his pocket for his cell phone without thinking. He needed to call the police. His stomach sank as he realized his wallet and cell phone had been in the pockets of his sports jacket. He imagined his credit card clenched in the bum's greasy fingers, currently paying for a new TV to hock on the street. He wanted to tear off the nasty coat and light it on fire as an act of petty revenge or maybe voodoo, but it was unusually cold for a December morning in Houston, and he didn't know how long he would have to be outside.

Jackson stumbled to the door, his feet stiff and throbbing. It was locked. He couldn't imagine all of the people just walking past him last night. Who would leave someone like him just slumped against a wall? Why wouldn't anyone help?

There was a corner drugstore open across the street. Jackson started moving toward it, trying not to think about how eerie everything looked in the light of the early morning. The blurry lights and neon glows of the evening before had been replaced by a dull, cloudy gray. The buildings looked shabby and old. He could see the trash lining the curbs. No one was walking the sidewalks. The air carried a faint scent of smoke, as if something far away had burned in the night and already been forgotten.

Jackson entered the drugstore and made his way through the tightly packed shelves to the checkout counter. The cashier was reading a celebrity gossip magazine and didn't bother to look up as he approached. Jackson wasn't used to being ignored and was more than a little angry at his current situation. He was ready to take it out on someone—especially a twenty-something morning cashier who was more interested in idiotic celebrities than someone's obvious distress.

With a firm slap of his palm against the counter, Jackson broke the cashier's concentration. The young man looked him up and down before motioning to a sign behind his head. NO LOITERING. He went back to reading his magazine.

"I'm not loitering," Jackson growled.

"So what do you want to buy?" the man asked without looking up.

"Well, nothing. I need help. I've been robbed."

"If you're not buying anything, then you're loitering."

"All my money was stolen along with my jacket. Do you really think I'd wear this . . . thing?"

"I've heard it before. We've got a strict no handout policy here, man. Sorry."

"Handout? I just need to call the police!"

"Phone's for paying customer's only."

Jackson blinked. "You think I'm homeless, don't you?"

The man looked up from his magazine with a frown. "Your status in life isn't my deal. My job is to look after *paying* customers."

"I can pay you. Let me use the phone to call the police, and I'll come back as soon as I get my money. I'll buy half this store!"

"Sir, you're going to have to leave now."

"GoCoNutty!"

"What?"

"That's my business! I'm Jackson Strong, cofounder and CEO of MadeStrong Inc.! I live at 147 Blue Bonnet Drive in he Woodlands. My phone number is . . ."

The man reached under his counter and came back up with a phone receiver. Jackson's heart leaped into his throat. "Thank—"

"Sir, if you don't leave this store in three seconds, I will have to call the police."

"Great! That's what I've been trying—"

"One."

"Tell them Jackson Strong is here and he's been robbed."

"Two."

Behind the cashier's head, Jackson noticed a novelty mirror. Red letters at the bottom poked through a film of dust and said, "Objects In Mirror May Be Dumber Than They Appear."

Jackson could barely make out his own reflection. His face and hair were covered with dirt, the gel long since giving up its hold to let his hair fall to the sides of his face in stringy wisps. The tan fake fur of his new coat poked past his cheek and seemed to tangle with his hair, giving him a wild look, like some new exotic animal at the zoo. That tiny glimpse shattered any confidence he still held, and it wasn't hard for him to imagine what might happen if the police showed up. Not even he would trust that reflection.

"Three."

Without a word, Jackson turned and made his way back through the shelves and out onto the street.

* * *

For a while he wandered the street, never straying too far from the bar. Part of him hoped that the bum would return to the scene of the crime to check up on him. Fantasies of violence and justice filled his mind, but there was no sign of the bum or his sports jacket.

Jackson had no sense of what time it was since he depended on his cell phone as a watch. He knew it was still early; that was easy to figure out by how quiet the city still was. He wondered if his ex-wife was still asleep. The past year of his life had been filled with all-nighters at work or with friends, so he hadn't really kept tabs on her. And now she was one of the only people he could think of that could rescue him. How long would it take her—or anyone—to realize he was missing? The thought froze the blood in his veins.

The only other person Jackson could think of was Matthew. Jackson replayed the movie of the night before in his mind. Matthew had left upset before he had decided to cross the street over to Gentleman's. No one knew where he was.

The thought sent a shiver through his body. He remembered a news story he had read once about a woman who was accidentally left behind by her dive boat at the Great Barrier Reef. When they finally realized their mistake, they raced back to the dive spot only to find her abandoned dive jacket. She was never found.

He was unmoored in unfamiliar waters. He needed to find a buoy.

CHAPTER 3

Taking a couple deep breaths, Jackson willed the panic back inside him, pushing it deep and covering it with his favorite mantra, "You've got this." He noticed that the streets were beginning to fill with bleary-eyed people holding newspapers and steaming cups of expensive coffee. Some were even dressed in suits. All of a sudden, they stopped being people to Jackson and turned into something else. Handholds. They were what he could use to get out of this horrible situation. He closed his eyes and visualized the people gathering around him to help. It was just a sale. He could do it.

Jackson opened his eyes and picked a young man in a tailored black suit. He walked straight for him, opening his mouth to speak, but the man just changed his own path in order to avoid him. The same thing happened with the next three people. It was as if Jackson were the villain in a new arcade game called Avoid the Bum.

Next he tried saying, "I'm not a bum," loudly as he approached, but that just made people avoid him with even more gusto. He thought about finding some cardboard and making a sign: "I'm a successful CEO who just got robbed.

Please help!" But just picturing it in his head was humiliating enough.

After fifteen minutes of unsuccessfully trying to get the attention of his peers, Jackson noticed a woman on the corner who seemed to be watching him. She was wearing a coat as bulky and awkward as his own, which helped him assume she was *actually* homeless. She waved at Jackson, and he turned away, hoping she got the point. Instead, she started waving harder and yelling, "Hey! You! Guy with the green coat!"

Every time she yelled, more people crossed the street to avoid him. He knew he had to talk to her, even if it was only to get her to stop acting like a crazy homeless person. Jackson half-jogged over to the corner and stood in front of the woman. Her coat had been a dark navy blue at one time, but now it was covered in dust and streaked by rain and humidity. At a distance, Jackson had assumed she was African-American, but up close he saw that her white skin was just tan and leathery, with creases worn in the surface. He tried not to stand too close, but the woman moved directly into his personal space while smiling widely. For one terrible second, he thought she was about to hug him, but instead she just laughed and said, "Honey, do you need help? You're acting kind of crazy."

Jackson snorted in surprise. "Me? Crazy?" He looked the woman up and down, raising his eyebrows. "When was the last time you looked in the mirror?"

"I fully know what I look like, thank you. It's a look I've earned. You, on the other hand, look like you're fresh out of the frying pan."

"I guess that's one way to put it."

"You just look like you need some help."

"Do you have a cell phone? Or some money for me to make a call?"

"If I did, I wouldn't be wasting your time chatting you up."

"So you're really just waving me over to point out the obvious. Thanks."

Jackson turned around to leave, but the woman caught his sleeve. He was reminded of the bum from the night before and had to stifle the urge to shove the lady away.

"I can help you get what you need," the woman said. "I know a thing or two."

Something dull and heavy started throbbing deep inside of Jackson. The woman stood looking at him expectantly, hand still on his forearm. He remembered a conversation he'd had a year previously with Bill Parsons, his old boss and mentor. MadeStrong had been facing a particularly tough month of sales. No one wanted to buy in to GoCoNutty. It seemed high risk because of the new pasteurization process. After listening to him vent over numerous cocktails, Bill had said, "Are you done whining now?"

"I am if that's what you want to call a retelling of the facts."

"Listen, Jackson. You're just learning what all of us had to learn at some point in our careers. You're pretty good with sales, right?"

"It's where I started."

Bill gave Jackson a hard look. "Then listen up. If you can do it yourself, do it."

The next month Jackson took personal control over the sales team, handling all the major potentials. He worked double shifts and didn't see his house for over a week straight, but the numbers started turning. Soon, they had the deals he could only dream of the month before.

Jackson thought of Bill Parsons standing in front of him, giving him that same hard look as he took in the olive green jacket and the fake fur. What was he thinking? That feeling inside of him was just the rolling waves of shame. Was he really about to accept help from this woman?

With a sharp tug, he was free from her grip. He crossed the street and started walking down the block, heading for an intersection he knew well. Soon he was free from the woman and her offers for help. His stomach started settling, and he gritted his teeth in determination. This was just a new challenge to overcome. A new adventure. And he didn't need anyone's help.

His target intersection was flooded with the foot traffic of Houston's downtown business elite. With a Starbucks on one corner and a bagel place across the street, it was the perfect spot to find a soul sensitive to his current hell.

He approached a woman who was somehow managing to text, drink coffee, and eat a bagel with just two hands. She didn't avoid him as he walked up to her, which was a good sign. Jackson cleared his throat.

"Excuse me."

The woman kept walking forward with her eyes glued to her phone. Jackson had to move out of the way to avoid being run over. He fell in step beside her.

"Excuse me," he tried again, a bit louder.

The woman looked up without slowing down. "Yes?"

Jackson realized at that moment that he didn't know what to do next. He had been so focused on just getting someone to pay attention to him that he had no idea how to ask for help. It was time to wing it.

"So last night I was downtown celebrating a new milestone in revenue with my business."

A slight downward curve appeared at the edges of the woman's mouth. Jackson was surprised he even noticed such a detail. He was used to saying his piece without having to worry about anyone's reaction.

"I know, I know, the coat. Just hear me out. So I was celebrating, and I think must have drank a little too much because—"

"Just ask me for money."

"What?"

"I don't know why you're telling me all of this when we both know you're just going to ask me for money."

The heat of shame started building in his stomach once more. "Can I have some money to make a phone call?"

"No. Sorry, my hands are full."

With that, the woman turned her attention back to her cellphone and left Jackson half a block away from the intersection, broke and ashamed.

He thought of Bill Parsons once more. Bill always had an answer for everything. His advice was usually somewhere between crotchety and mean, but he was successful at everything he touched, so Jackson assumed he knew what he was talking about. He closed his eyes and imagined Bill in his mind. He pictured himself seated at his refinished antique oak business desk with Bill on the other side. What would Bill say to him in a situation like this?

"So what, you failed," Bill would say with a scowl. "Can you blame her? Look at your ridiculous coat."

"At least it's warm," Jackson would answer.

"Don't fool yourself."

"So how am I supposed to do this? I can't even muster enough compassion in these people to listen to me for five seconds, let alone give me the change in their pockets."

"You already know what I'm gonna say. If you want to get better at this, you've got to just do it some more. You'll get better with time."

It was the same advice he'd given Jackson at the very beginning of MadeStrong and GoCoNutty. A variation on the whole "practice makes perfect" line adored by every one of his high school gym teachers.

"Just do it some more," Jackson told himself. He opened his eyes and immediately picked out a young man in a purple tie from the crowd of commuters. This time he would cut right to the chase.

"Excuse me," Jackson said once the young man made eye contact.

"Yeah?"

"Do you have any change you can spare? I need to make a phone call."

"Sorry, I'm strictly debit card these days. No change."

It was an excuse Jackson had frequently used himself, so he couldn't really fault the man. But after the fourth person in a row used it, he was ready to swear off debit cards for life. Or sue Visa.

Bill's advice didn't seem too effective in the current situation. Jackson could feel the panic fighting to claw its way out from the pit of his stomach. He was in over his head and every lifeline was out of reach. That's when his luck changed for the first time in twelve hours. Jackson saw someone he recognized.

It was a lawyer who worked on another floor in their office complex. At least, he *looked* like it. Jackson couldn't be absolutely sure since the extent of their interactions had been to occasionally compare weekend stories or comment on current events whenever they crossed paths in the elevator. They weren't friends, but he was pretty sure he knew the man's name. It was as if heaven had opened its gates and sent the man floating serenely to the ground to save him.

"Frank!" Jackson said as he crossed the street to greet him.

The man looked up and around tentatively. His glance brushed right over Jackson.

"Frank!" This time there was no hesitation. The man looked up and locked eyes with him. He frowned.

"It's me, Frank. Jackson Strong, from the building. Don't mind the coat."

"How do you know my name?"

The menace with which Frank growled out the question stopped Jackson instantly. "I . . . I just told you. We work in the same building."

"You've got the wrong Frank, I think."

"You work on the 3rd floor of the Pinecroft building. Dalhouse, Davis, and Jentz."

"Have you been following me?"

"What? No. It's Jackson. I work there, too. MadeStrong. 5th floor. I've been robbed, and I need your help."

"I don't know how you figured all of this out, but you need to turn around and walk away. I don't want to see your face again."

"But—"

Frank pulled out his phone. "Or I can call the police."

Jackson let his shoulders fall. Defeated. He slumped away from Frank, certain that it was a sign from up high that he was in a purgatory that would never end.

"That was awkward." Jackson almost jumped out of his coat at the voice. It was right beside him. He looked past his shoulder and down to see the same wrinkled face from earlier. It was the old woman in the blue coat. "After watching that, I don't care what you think. I *know* you need my help."

"I've got this," Jackson said.

"Honey, the only thing you've got is that coat on your back and a one-way ticket to the holding pen if you keep it up. I don't know who made you so afraid of asking for help, but you should know they did you a pretty big disservice."

The woman standing before him was as opposite from Bill Parsons as a person could get. In fact, she was one step away from having a smell you could see. But in that moment Jackson realized there was another key difference between Bill Parsons and the woman—one that had nothing to do with appearance. The woman was in front of him, offering help, and Bill Parsons was a man whose advice didn't seem to translate to Jackson's current situation.

"What's your name?" Jackson asked.

"My friends call me Mercy."

"I'm Jackson."

"Well, Jackson, let me tell you what I notice. You've got that do-it-yourself, I-can-do-anything attitude that comes natural to people like the ones you've been asking for money. I know you got that coat and that strained look, but I'd say this is the first time you've ever had to ask someone for money."

For a brief moment, Jackson didn't say anything out of fear of who might be listening. But the crowd just surged past them, consumed by their own lives, bagels, coffee, and cellphones. "It's that obvious?"

Mercy laughed. "I've gotten pretty good at reading people. It's how to survive out here. And you're terrible at it."

Jackson couldn't believe he was being laughed at. "Well, it's not like I've had any practice! I prefer making real money, not chump change. I bet I could get good at it if this was my life."

"Honey, whoever made you think you can just do it all yourself was flat out wrong. With that attitude, you wouldn't last a day out here." Mercy was still smiling, but there was something hard in her voice. "Not a single day."

"So what makes you the expert," Jackson asked, "despite the obvious?"

"You can keep up the attitude all you want. I'm still going to speak some truth over you because you need it. I'm going to tell you about my mother."

"Your mother?" Jackson couldn't imagine the day getting any weirder.

"Yes, my mother. I've got my own people floating through my head, reminding me of the way to do things, just like you. My mother owned her own cleaning service for a number of years. She was good at cleaning up restaurants, bars, that sort of thing. It wasn't the best money, but we got by. But then all these cleaning companies started showing up in town. They were stealing business from her left and right. So she did what all of us would do, she started working harder. But guess what happened? She kept losing business and grew more exhausted. That was her wakeup call that she needed to take a risk and think differently. Most of us get that wakeup call at certain key points in our life, but it takes guts to follow through. If we're honest, it's a lot easier to just keep doing things the way we've been doing them. Changing our approach usually begins with honestly admitting where we've gone wrong."

Jackson thought about all the people who'd just turned him down. He had been at it all morning, at least a couple of hours, and had nothing to show for it. It was one of his longest losing streaks in recent memory. Yet he'd convinced himself to go it alone and just keep doing the same thing over and over again. "So how did your mother change?"

"She had to step back and look at her business with clear eyes. She had been assuming that it was her team's cleaning skills that would win her business. But there was no way to compete with the larger teams and better equipment of the new companies. She asked one of her clients why they were sticking with her, and they said it was because she was familiar and they liked her. That's when it clicked for my mom. She started focusing on customer service rather than their cleaning skills. She trained her team in how to figure out what personal touches each of their clients enjoyed and how to make a nightly clean into something a bit more personal. It could be a cleaner with a certain scent or a way to fold hand towels. She went out of her way to make sure her customers felt special and respected. Soon she was swimming in clients, many of them ones who'd been left feeling cold by the other cleaning companies. That was a good stage in life for us all."

Mercy paused in her story, and Jackson thought he saw water welling in the corners of her eyes. He wondered what had happened in her life that she would end up in that big blue coat, offering help to someone like him. He figured it wasn't a very tactful question to ask at the moment. To his surprise, he didn't feel as ashamed to be talking with her as he did at first. She told a good story. "Your mom sounds like a smart businesswoman," he said.

"She was. Instilled that same sense of kindness in me as well. Practically forced it into me."

"I've noticed." There was a tiny pinch of guilt in his chest as Jackson thought about how he'd treated her just minutes before, how she shrugged it off and opened up to him.

The woman turned to sneeze into the sleeve of her jacket, but Jackson saw that she was really wiping her eyes. He was never good at comforting anyone, so instead he said, "So you think I need to change my thinking?"

"Is that the right question?"

Jackson winced. He didn't want to say it, but there was no one around, and, to his embarrassment, he was actually interested in what Mercy had to say. "How do *you* think I should change my thinking in this situation?"

Mercy laughed into her sleeve. "Oh boy. That's the one. You've got a lot to change."

"Thanks. That's a confidence booster."

"First, you gotta stop asking for help from *your* people."

"*My* people?"

Mercy waved her arm at the crowd. "How many of these people look like you in normal life?"

"All of them."

"And how many times have you given help to someone who asked for it on the street."

"Around—"

"Be honest."

"Never."

"Exactly. You've been asking for help from the people who will never give it. You're not even on the same plane of existence. You might as well be from some parallel universe looking like you do."

"I get it. No need to go science fiction on me. So who should I be looking for?"

"You've got to find the people who see you as a human being. Someone who can imagine what it's like for you. Someone who will look at you like you have a soul."

"How can you tell?"

"Different ways. Usually it's the ones who will make eye

contact with you first. It's all in their eyes. There will be some kindness there; they won't turn away from you. They might even smile at you."

"Look at you, friendly eyes, smiles—got it." Jackson turned to start searching for the ideal person in the crowd.

"Hold on, now," Mercy said.

"I've got this."

"There it is again. That phrase. You've probably got to unlearn that one. I know being all can-do is great in your world, but there's something else I learned from my mother."

Although he really just wanted to get on with finding the right person, by now Jackson knew better than to ignore a story about Mercy's mom. "I'm all ears," he said.

"Looking like that, you're all *coat* and ears," Mercy laughed. "My mother had this thing about cleaning floors," Mercy continued. "She would spend all this time on them, especially the tile floors of the Tex-Mex places. She would scrub the grout and make sure each tile was as clean as one of their plates. The problem was it took her forever to do. We started seeing her less and less at home. It wasn't until some of her clients expressed dissatisfaction that she caught on to what was happening."

"Wait, her clients were *dissatisfied* with her attention to detail?"

"It wasn't so much the quality of work; it was the time it would take her. She spent so much time on those floors that she didn't have as much time to chat with the cooks, dishwashers, and managers of the restaurants. She realized that her most valuable skill was the gift of sociable gab, but instead she was pouring all her time into cleaning the floors. She needed to value her time. She even thought about it in terms of money. She put an hourly rate on her time and realized that it would actually cost less to hire another team member to clean the floors. That's what she did, and soon they were able to add more clients thanks to the relationships she developed with some of the managers."

"I get it. I need to value my time. But I don't see the point right now. All I've got is time, at least until I can get some money."

"The point is sometimes it's all right to let someone else do the work for you." Mercy smiled at him and cracked her knuckles.

"That someone else is you, right?"

"You catch on quick."

Before he could protest, Mercy was out in the crowd. He watched her big blue coat flutter through the people. Then her arm shot straight into the air, and her fingers started wiggling in his direction. She was waving him over.

Jackson sheepishly trudged to where she was waiting with a big smile. There was another woman standing next to her. She looked to be around Jackson's age, but her clothes were rumpled and she had dark shadows under her eyes. She looked right at Jackson as he approached and smiled. "Mercy told me you need some help," she said.

He was taken aback by the kindness in her voice. It was the complete opposite of the gruff indifference he'd been hearing for most of the day. "Believe it or not," he said, "I'm a pretty successful businessman. I was robbed last night and just need some money to make a few calls."

"I believe it," the woman said. "That coat's not your style. I don't want to be offensive or anything, but you look like a kid playing dress-up in his dad's clothes."

"That's probably the nicest thing I've heard all day."

The woman giggled. "How much do you need?"

She ended up giving Jackson five dollars and telling him she'd pray for his safety. She hugged Mercy and then disappeared back into the crowd. Jackson felt a lump in the back of his throat and discovered that he actually felt a little moved.

"I can tell you feel it," Mercy said. "It's a good feeling to be seen."

They made their way to a friendly convenience store Mercy knew of. Jackson bought her a coffee and then made his way to a payphone in the back of the store. It wasn't until he dropped the first quarters in that he realized he didn't know who he should call. He realized that he had next to no one in his life with the same kindness or compassion of the two women he just met. He wanted to get home. He started with Karen, but she didn't pick up. He left a message with the number of the payphone and asked her to call him back as soon as possible. Then he called Matthew and ended up leaving the same message. He considered calling Bill Parsons but realized that he probably wouldn't even help. He'd just expect Jackson to figure it out on his own—to visualize the win.

As he waited for one of them to call back, he debated whether he should call the police. He was certain his cash was already gone, and his credit cards could be cancelled easily. He didn't want to sit in a police station filing report after report. He wanted to put all of this behind him.

After an hour of waiting by the payphone, Mercy came and found him. "Are you OK, honey?"

"No one's calling back."

She handed him a cup of coffee and put a hand on his arm. She snapped her fingers in an exaggerated "a-ha!" and reached deep into one of the pockets of her coat. She pulled out a flyer and passed it to Jackson. Big, bold letters spelled out **The Lot** across the front of the paper. Underneath, it read, "Services every Friday from 6-9 PM. Free snacks and coffee. Meet at the empty lot at the corner of Sandusky and Freight St."

"What's this?"

"This is a place that helps, especially when you're extra distressed."

"Is it nearby?"

"It's a walk, but I think you've got it in you."

"Are you gonna take me there?"

Mercy just smiled. "This is where I leave you," she said. She spent the next few minutes giving Jackson detailed instructions on how to reach the empty lot.

"Maybe I should wait here in case someone calls back," Jackson said when she was done.

Mercy looked him up and down. "That jacket sure has a lot of pockets," she said.

"What?"

"I mean, there's got to be nine or ten on there."

It was true. The jacket was very utilitarian in its placement of pockets. Jackson just didn't see how it was relevant.

Mercy reached out and snapped open the left breast pocket of the jacket. She pretended to reach in and pull something out, pinched between her fingers. But she wasn't holding anything.

"OK . . ." Jackson said.

"I'm a visual person, Jackson, and I get the feeling you are too."

She really is good at reading people, he thought, nodding at her to continue and wondering what the point of all this was.

"I think we're a lot like that jacket of yours. We're made up of pockets. And when people give us advice, or we learn something new, we put it into one of those pockets. It sits there waiting for us to pull it out and remember it. Problem is, sometimes we put some bad advice in our pockets." She held her pinched fingers in front of Jackson. "That's what this is. Bad advice. Do it yourself. Just keep doing it."

Mercy showed Jackson her other hand, with the same pinched fingers. "This is the good advice. Tried-and-tested by my mother and by us. I'm going to put that into your pocket so you can carry it with you.

"**Don't be afraid to think differently and ask for help**," Mercy said as she snapped the pocket closed.

As weird as it was to admit, Jackson knew the old homeless

woman was right. And it was the first time that morning that he didn't absolutely hate the coat he was stuck in. Before he even knew what he was doing, he gave her a big hug. "I can't wait here all day," he said, willing to change his strategy. "I'll go look for help at The Lot."

"And I'll wait here to help out," Mercy said. "If anyone calls, I'll let them know where you're going."

Downtown Houston felt different as Jackson left the convenience store. The air didn't feel as cold and the hustle and bustle of the morning commuters had died to a thin trickle. He no longer felt panicked or hopeless. He thought of Mercy and the new advice in his pocket. Then he began his journey to The Lot—the mysterious place that helps.

CHAPTER 4

It took Jackson a while to figure out why he was feeling so stressed out by Mercy's directions. He thought she was clear enough when she told him the way to The Lot, but he realized after walking a couple of blocks that his comfort with the directions was based on the false assumption that he had his bearings. He was used to navigating the clean roadways of the northern suburbs, where nearly every road led to a county road or highway 45. In the heart of the city, everything looked a little different.

He was still downtown, that much was obvious from the sparkling towers of glass surrounding him—home to banks, big oil, and investment firms. For a moment he considered finding his way to the MadeStrong offices, but picturing walking past his employees broken, haggard, and dressed in a ridiculous, ratty coat made him want to throw up. Besides, his employees needed confidence in him right before Nighthawk's launch. They couldn't afford to see their fearless CEO looking like an extra from some Charles Dickens miniseries.

Instead, he kept walking block after block. Soon, he was

totally lost. He made a series of right turns and passed by a law firm twice. Unless there were different offices of the same firm. He needed to escape the heart of downtown—that much was clear from Mercy's directions. She had explained that The Lot was on the border of the older section of The Heights. He knew the hip, new part of The Heights pretty well since it was where young professionals went to drink. But he had no idea how to get to the old, less hip part. He thought about asking one of the people trying to avoid him on the sidewalk. But he could tell from their finely groomed facial hair and expensive haircuts that they would only know the hip section.

Jackson imagined having a bird's-eye view of the city, and that was when he understood why he felt so stressed. The map he imagined, with its bisected blocks and different colored buildings, looked just like a Rubik's cube. He had always hated Rubik's cubes. It was the one game he had never been able to master growing up. He even resorted one time to peeling every sticker and painstakingly reattaching them to give off the illusion of victory. His mom was impressed, but he just felt hollow and ashamed. As if that threatened to derail him. He had felt some momentum with Mercy—a glimmer of hope. But now he was stuck in a Rubik's cube and would surely be defeated.

Jackson randomly turned down a side street, thankful for a moment's escape from the towering monuments of success and wealth. That street led to another, then another. Soon he had left the skyscrapers and had entered a kind of shaggy dog residential area. The homes were small, ranch-style one stories with fences in varying states of decay. The people on the sidewalks changed from the young and beautiful to the old and haggard. Jackson still didn't register much attention though. As he walked deeper into the heart of the neighborhood, more buildings and homes started to look abandoned. One house was leaning so much that he probably could have tipped it over with his pinky. The people didn't fare better. Some of them looked to be decaying as well. Jackson stopped thinking of his jacket as an impediment. Instead, it became a necessary disguise. He didn't know what would happen if he were found out, but it probably wouldn't be all that good for his health.

Panicked and lost, he made another turn and was surprised to discover a quiet block of locally owned businesses. There was a hardware store named The Tool Shed and an auto shop obviously named after its owner, Mr. G. But it was the building at the end of the block that stopped him in his tracks and made him forget all about his childhood defeat by color-coded cubes. There, on a quiet street in the dilapidated ghetto, surrounded on all sides by decaying warehouses and homes, was an art gallery.

Rose Tinted Glasses was spray painted in red over a black background next to the storefront's window. The window displayed a giant photograph of a jungle village somewhere in South America. It was full of vibrant greens and browns, mixing with the yellows, reds, and blues of the clothes the people were wearing. Jackson usually didn't have much time for art, unless it was the opening of an exhibit where he could do some networking, but that oversized photo stopped him in his tracks. There was some ethereal light it captured that he couldn't quite place, as if everything in the photograph was glowing at once, but the source of the light would disappear as soon as he tried to focus on it. Jackson was so engrossed by the jungle scene that he almost missed the piece of paper taped up to its right.

It was the same flyer he held in his hands.

Time for a shortcut, he thought. After all, if the art gallery was somehow affiliated with The Lot, couldn't they just help him right here? He could end his journey early and get back to CEOing by nightfall.

Jackson opened the door and entered the gallery under

the twinkling of a door chime. It was a tune he instantly recognized from his youth. Blondie's *Heart of Glass*. The room was an open square with various pieces of art all around the walls. Most of it was photographs: scenes from other countries and beautiful close-ups of what Jackson assumed was the surrounding neighborhood. There were also some large pieces of repurposed wood covered in flowing, vibrant graffiti script. They held messages like "Look close enough to find beauty," "Desk jobs are for zombies," and "There's no stopping a punk rock heart." The latter also featured a stenciled illustration of a heart with a mohawk giving a thumbs-down to a sad looking set of defibrillators.

There was a tiny counter to one side covered in what Jackson assumed were band stickers. It held an ancient cash register, some flyers for local concerts and events, and, sitting behind it with a look stuck halfway between annoyance and interest, was the artist herself.

She looked to be in her 30's, although her choice of attire definitely made her seem younger. She was dressed all in black, complete with a black leather jacket that would be right at home on the back of a Harley chopper. Her hair was cut in a 60's bob and was dyed bright red. *She sure looks like an artist,* Jackson thought.

"You sure look like you're homeless," the artist said. *Touché.*

"Just kind of?" Jackson asked.

"Well, you have the right attire. That coat looks like it's been to Bora Bora and back, but you don't have the right face. It's not a homeless face."

"Pretty perceptive."

"I also can tell you're not here to buy my art," the woman continued.

Jackson shrugged sheepishly. "I don't have any money. In fact, that's why I stopped in. I noticed you have a flyer up for The Lot."

"I help out there from time to time."

"A new friend named Mercy pointed me in their direction. She said it's the best place to get help."

"Aww, I *love* Mercy! She sure pointed you in the right direction."

"So I noticed you had the flyer up," Jackson said, "and I figured you must help out or know The Lot in some way. And since you said it yourself that it's a place to find help—"

"Hold on just a minute," the woman interrupted.

She pointed to what looked like an old cabinet door behind her head, covered in graffiti. Jackson didn't know how he had missed the giant flowing letters that spelled out "The only help I give is advice and free coffee."

"I've owned this place for half a decade. That was made with years of experience, my friend. I've heard every tall tale that could ever be told. It's easier to stick to my guns rather than to try to sift out what's true."

It was pragmatic and clever, which bugged Jackson even more. "Can I get that coffee then?" he asked.

"Of course . . . what's your name again?"

"It's Jackson."

"And I'm Rose. Why don't you tell me your story as I make you a cup."

Jackson's annoyance at not getting the help he imagined quickly dissipated as he watched Rose make his coffee. A true artist, she did not settle for a carafe of drip burning on the percolator for half the day. Instead, as Jackson related his story, she hand ground the beans, brought the water to a temperature-controlled boil in a goose neck kettle, and brewed the coffee using a well-traveled French press. She pulled two old reupholstered chairs out of a back room into the gallery for them to sit on. The cup she eventually placed in front of him was a dark, velvety masterpiece. It was the best coffee he had ever tasted.

"It's good, right?" Rose said with a grin.

"Good doesn't do it justice. Divine, celestial, pour-me-another—anything but good."

"So you're telling me that underneath all that dirt, grime, and ugly jacket, you're the guy who invented GoCoNutty."

Jackson was about to take all the credit, but it didn't seem right. He was already at his absolute worst point in life in front of this woman. He had nothing to prove. "Actually, it was my business partner Matthew's idea. I just helped bring it to fruition."

"Well, I can tell you that I've heard a lot of stories in my time here, but yours is one of the craziest."

"Crazy but true!"

"I withhold judgment. When offering coffee and advice, I really don't have to decide the truth of someone's story. I can just listen. It's nice."

For the next few minutes they sat in silence, enjoying their coffee. Jackson gazed out on all of the artwork and tried to pinpoint what he was feeling. He knew that he should have felt annoyed and impatient with not receiving the help he expected from Rose, but he couldn't work himself up. It was as if all the stress and anxiety was untwisting inside of him like an unraveling ball of yarn. Staring into a photograph of a flat green field in the middle of a mountainous jungle, Jackson pinpointed what he was feeling. For the first time in a long time, he felt peaceful.

"I have a question for you," Jackson said as Rose refilled his cup.

"No, I don't dye my hair to go along with my name. It's strictly a coincidence!"

"Interesting, but not my question."

"I just figured from your choice of attire that it would be a fashion question."

"Nice. So you won't help, but you feel completely fine with making light of someone's worst-case scenario."

"Humor's like the friend who always has your back."

Jackson pointed to one of the spray-painted pieces of wood. "I think that should be your next slogan."

Rose smiled. "Perfect! I'll make sure the profits of the sale go back into the coffee fund in honor of you."

"Not into my pocket?"

"You know the policy. Now what's your question?"

"How does an art gallery on the edge of the ghetto stay in business?"

"Now *that's* a question. We may need another pot of coffee."

Jackson tugged at his new jacket. "In case you didn't notice, I've got plenty of time."

Rose nodded and chuckled. "After I graduated art school, I spent the next couple of years living cheaply and traveling the world. I loved photography and wanted to take as many pictures of other cultures as possible. Through selling some of the photographs, I was able to travel to Peru, Zambia, Argentina, India, Sri Lanka, Turkey, South Africa, Australia, and New Zealand. I quickly realized that maintaining that lifestyle was impossible. I came home to Houston ready to settle into a more sustainable career."

"Still in art?"

"Of course. It's my passion and the source of all my skills. I was smart enough to recognize that and take the risks necessary to live as an artist."

"Did you ever try graphic design?"

Rose gave Jackson a slight frown. "I said an artist, not a creative. I had lots of friends who went that route and found a good career, but I knew it wasn't for me. I think it's important to recognize the life you want for yourself and then go after it. I knew the risks involved in living as an artist and the sacrifices I would have to make. But I wasn't afraid."

Jackson thought of the very beginning of MadeStrong, when it was just him and Matthew creating business plans in local coffee shops. It was risky, but they both had just *known* they had to do it. They were living directly in the middle of their skill sets, sacrificing security and salary at the beginning, but never compromising. "I know what you mean," he said.

"Right. So I opened my first art gallery in the hip part of The Heights, right next to a new record store and coffee shop. It was the perfect location. I had my art on the walls, a studio in the back, and a small kitchen where I could brew my coffee. I could work my own hours, determine my own priorities, and I didn't need to have any meetings! It seemed like it was going to be bliss. I hired a friend to help me manage the sales in the gallery, another friend to organize events, and a third to help with marketing and making prints of photographs and paintings. It was supposed to be my dream—working for myself."

"The shared dream of every entrepreneur, myself included."

Rose raised her eyebrows as if to say, *I'm still not sure.* Then she continued. "But it was a nightmare. After a year, I was completely exhausted. My visions of streamlined workdays and 3-day weekends had turned into bags under my eyes and a desk filled with empty coffee mugs. My employees were all brilliant artists in their own right, but they couldn't seem to capture my vision for what I wanted the gallery to be. I had always imagined an urban gallery that was really a series of windows into other worlds. I wanted people to enter and completely forget that they were in the city. I wanted them to have a liminal experience."

Jackson held up his hand. "Wait, what's a liminal experience?"

"It's a term that comes from anthropology. In rituals, it's the time when the participant is at the threshold of change. They are no longer the person they were when they started the ritual, but they are not yet the person they will be once the ritual is complete. So it's like this transition state when endless possibilities of change can happen. Like, you're no longer set in your ways. You can suddenly imagine a new future for yourself."

Jackson thought of summer camps when he was a kid. How they always seemed to be a place to test out new facets of his identity. A place he could be someone new because no one knew him. And how he always felt different at the end of the summer when he returned home, a feeling that he was not quite the same person who had slept in his bedroom a month earlier. "I think I'm following," he said.

"So my vision for the gallery was for people to come in and have this otherworldly experience. I wanted them to step through my photographs of other cultures like windows and have their urban or suburban mindset thrown a little out-of-whack. I wanted them to leave a little different than they came in."

"Sounds like a cool vision."

"I thought so. The problem was explaining it in concrete terms to my crew. It was so clear in my head that I thought it should be obvious. But my employees kept making all these decisions that seemed to oppose my vision. Like, my marketer kept trying to play up the ironic aspects of my art in order to bring in the hipsters. And my events coordinator would set up these nights that had more to do with social networking than experiencing the beauty of another culture through art. So I started doing parts of their job for them as well. It was easier than always having to try to explain what I didn't like about the work they were doing. I didn't want to frustrate them. Instead of having the work schedule of my dreams, I was chained to a never-ending train of duties."

Rose paused, and Jackson realized she was gauging him for a reaction—a test to see if he could relate on some entrepreneurial level. He recognized that he could. He thought of the endless nights at the office spent correcting other employees' work. No one ever seemed to grasp how important even the littlest details were to any product they delivered. He always felt as if he had to go over the same processes over and over with the same people. It was time consuming and made him feel like Sisyphus endlessly pushing his boulder up a hill. But he didn't want Rose to know all of that. He didn't really think of it as a weakness. His mentors had been very clear from the start—owning your own business meant a life of working extra hours and cleaning up the messes of others. "Sounds like owning your own business," he said.

"That's what I thought. After all, it was my name and my art, so any failure would be forever attached to me on a personal level. Luckily, one of my employees recognized I was about to have a total, Richter scale meltdown and referred me to a friend who was a business coach—what?"

Jackson suddenly grasped that his inward frown was also on his face. "Nothing. It's just you're the second one to mention a business coach to me in the last 24 hours. I'm not much of a fan."

"Three things, Jackson. One—that's like saying you're not a fan of wisdom or learning. Two—if your story's to be believed, maybe you should take note. And three—this is my story—no more frowning!"

"Touché."

"It's the price of admission. Anyways, I ended up meeting with the business coach, and he listened to my long list of complaints. Then he asked, 'What do you need to do to make your business run without you?' It blew my mind, and I kind of flipped out a bit. He explained that I had bought into the delusion that an entrepreneur needs to be a workaholic. He helped me remember my original reasons for wanting to go into business for myself: freedom and autonomy. I wanted the free time to explore my passions. He said that a business should be created and molded to give me an amazing life— one that allows me to live out my life purpose. Then he said something that I still carry around with me."

Jackson thought that Rose was speaking metaphorically until she reached into her pocket and unfolded a piece of paper to hand to him. A sentence was sketched into the paper with the same flowing calligraphy of the graffiti art. Jackson read it out loud. "You should *work* as little as possible so that you can *live* as much as possible."

"With his help, I realized that working as little as possible wasn't lazy or apathetic. Instead, it was the mark of a great leader. I was overworking myself because of a failure to communicate my vision. What I saw as no one being able to do the work as well as I could was in reality no one clearly understanding what was expected of them. I set about writing down my vision and some processes for how to complete tasks like marketing and event planning while maintaining the vision. Soon, my crew was knocking it out of the park every day. I found that I could spend the entire day in my studio creating without having to worry about the day-to-day tasks of the gallery. And it was successful. Soon people were buying more art than ever before, which allowed me to travel more than I ever dreamed. I was *working* less but *living* more!"

Something nagged at Jackson, making him feel as if he wanted to stand up and leave. It was a strong reaction, and it took him a moment to place the feeling as jealousy. He wanted what Rose was describing. MadeStrong had been his life, but at its heart it was still work. He tried to think back about some of his dreams at the beginning, what he wanted to do with his life, but it was too fuzzy. Everything seemed crushed under the weight of long hours and needing to be the one in charge.

"I still have that gallery in The Heights, and its success let me open up this one. I discovered a new facet of my vision when I had the time and room to breathe. I found a new desire to bring art into poverty. Part of it was from spending time with The Lot and meeting all of these truly artistic souls living in poverty. So I opened up this place and began giving photography lessons on donated cameras. Most of the pictures you see weren't taken by me. And their sales go right back to the artist and the community."

Jackson looked around the gallery once more with new

eyes. The urban poverty on display was not decrepit or depressing. Every photograph featured something beautiful, as if the photographer was proving that you could find God in even the least valued object. He felt as if new lenses were being placed over his eyes, giving him a new capacity for beauty, even in the midst of poverty. It was a liminal experience.

Rose just smiled and said, "You feel it, don't you?"

"I do."

"That business coach saved my gallery and my career. I never would have thought working as little as possible could be the mark of a great leader."

Jackson just sat in silence, trying to take it all in. He felt parts of his heart stretching, ready to take in this new wisdom. But he wasn't sure he needed it. His business was successful enough already. What he needed was a shower, a change of clothes, and to be back home.

Rose seemed to sense this and said, "Coffee and advice. That's my deal. But for being a great listener, I'll give you a bonus."

"A ride to the suburbs?"

"Hey, I might work less now, but I'm still on the clock. Let me see that flyer." Rose took The Lot flyer from Jackson, flipped it over, and started drawing him a map. "You've wandered pretty far off-track right now, but luckily my artistic skills translate into some pretty good map making. You'll want to follow this closely, especially until you're out of this neighborhood. You don't want to end up on a street like King Street. You're too much of a rookie for it."

She passed the map back to Jackson who took it and studied her sketch. It really was easy to read, even for a newbie on the streets.

"You know, I'm going to The Lot tonight. You could just hang out here and we could go together. I usually leave around 6," Rose said.

Jackson glanced at the clock. It was just after noon. "I'd

rather get there earlier and just put an end to my little Alice in Wonderland experience."

"Well, good luck then! And don't forget my free advice."

Jackson could almost see Rose's words floating in front of him, written in the same graffiti font as the art covering the walls: **Work less so you can live more.** He imagined putting them in the pocket right below the one already holding Mercy's advice. "I just put it in my pocket," he said.

Rose raised her eyebrows and laughed. "You've got plenty of those, I guess."

"Why don't you graffiti it onto some wood like those other sayings?"

Rose chewed on her lower lip and furrowed her brow. Then she answered, "There's just some things that are meant to be carried around with you. For me it's not a momentary reminder sort of thing—it's a constant."

Jackson tried to conjure up his own constants. He couldn't think of any. All he saw were work and revenue. But now he had a dirty, threadbare jacket with two pockets full of thoughts to carry around.

"It was nice getting to drink some coffee with you, Jackson," Rose said. "Hopefully I'll see you tonight."

Jackson waved goodbye and exited the gallery. He glanced at his new map, took a left, and started walking. He was worriedly mulling over what Rose had meant by *hopefully* when something caught his eye and made him stop in his tracks.

Two blocks in front of him, weaving in between people on the sidewalk, was a flicker from his former life—a Navy Brooks Brothers sport coat, standing out against the dilapidated urban backdrop.

It was the man who had robbed him.

CHAPTER 5

Jackson took off down the block. His heavy coat thumped against his knees with every lunge of his legs, threatening to tangle him up and tumble him down the sidewalk. He pulled the sides of his jacket up, freeing his knees to pump, not caring if he looked like a schoolgirl holding her dress up to cross a puddle.

The chase was pure impulse. It was a reaction to seeing his coat—earned with *his* hard work and money—parading down the street on the back of someone who had stolen from him with no second thought. Jackson didn't know what he would do when he caught the man. For a split second he fantasized an epic street fight in which he furiously punched the man's lights out, but he knew his lack of experience meant it was only a dream. He considered just grabbing the man and holding onto him until he could convince someone to call the police. He wasn't sure if anyone in the neighborhood would be willing to help, but he had to try. The fact that he could see the man casually walking just a block ahead of him had to mean something. Justice was being delivered into his hands.

Suddenly, the man turned left in the middle of the block.

"Hey!" Jackson yelled, trying to stall him or turn him around. Some of the pedestrians and loiterers twisted at the force of his voice, but the man had already disappeared. Jackson pushed his body to run even faster, ignoring his aching muscles and lungs.

He reached the spot where the man had vanished and slowed to a stop. It was a dark alley between two gutted and abandoned warehouses. The high walls of the buildings blocked most of the sunlight, leaving the alley in shadows. Jackson squinted his eyes but couldn't see more than a couple of feet into the darkness. The man who robbed him was in there somewhere. Jackson didn't have time for fear.

"I just want to talk to you for a minute," Jackson said once he caught his breath. He was impressed with how sincere and calm he sounded. There was no hint of the rage seething in his veins. He took a step into the alley, watching the shadows climb from his foot up his leg to his waist. With a deep breath, he stepped all the way in.

The first thing Jackson noticed when he was fully engulfed by the alley was the fact that there were a million places to hide. Old pallets of wood lined the right side, while the left had multiple doorways cut into the side of the decaying warehouse. Trash littered the whole thing, punctuating each step with a crinkle or snap. He strained to take in all the different nooks and crannies, ready to fight or run whenever the man appeared.

Then the alley abruptly ended. The back wall of another building blocked his path. It was a dead end. Jackson reached the wall and turned to scan the alley again. How could the man have just disappeared?

To his right, he noticed an overturned bottle of beer. It was still spilling its stale liquid. Someone had knocked it over—recently. He moved closer to inspect it. That's when he noticed the gap. It was a gap of about three feet between the building on the right and the back building. He remembered playing hide-and-seek with his cousins in one of the older industrial wards in Milwaukee—how the old buildings often didn't share walls when they were back to back, but instead had tiny gaps perfect for sliding into. He hadn't noticed the gap immediately because it was even darker than the alley he was in and his eyes were still adjusting to the shadows. It looked big enough to squeeze into if you were interested in getting stuck in a terrifying place no one could ever find you.

But the man had gone into the gap. There was no other explanation. Jackson did a full 360 scan of the alley once more, just to be sure the homeless man wasn't lurking in a doorway praying he would go into the gap and get stuck. Then he sucked in his gut, turned sideways, and wedged himself into the gap.

He scraped his back and his belly farther into the darkness. Something dripped on his head, and he forcibly willed himself to ignore it. His arms were locked into place on either side of his body, so there was nothing he could do about it. He tried not to imagine his expensive sports jacket sliding against the dirty brick of the building in front of him.

"Hello," Jackson called out. The sound of his voice was dampened by the tight space. "I'm not going to hurt you or anything. I just want my phone and my jacket back." Silence. He kept skidding his body down into the crevice when he realized a change in his surroundings, behind his back. The wall of the front building continued, but the back building ended. Another wall started about three feet in front of it, creating another similar gap. Jackson made the turn and started pushing his way through the new crack. This one was different. Light flooded into it from some place ahead. Jackson strained for the light, ready to get out of the confined fissure between buildings. He scrambled and scraped his way forward, trying not to panic. Finally, he pushed his way out of the crevice and into the light.

He found himself in a new neighborhood of one-story ranch homes that dead-ended at the wall of the old warehouses he had broken free from. It would have been interchangeable with the suburban neighborhood Jackson grew up in, except that every house on the block had iron bars over their windows and front doors. Not a good sign. Jackson scanned the block for the man with his coat, but he had disappeared. He wasn't sure the man had even exited into this neighborhood in the first place. The only people he could see was a group of young Hispanic men huddled together at the end of the block. Some of them were on bikes and others were holding what looked like basketballs. A few were smoking. All of them had turned to look at Jackson.

He felt a sudden impulse to wave, but stifled it. The crowd didn't look like the waving type. They looked like the kind of people you didn't want to notice you. Two of the young men broke off from the pack and started striding toward Jackson. The rest of the crowd cheered and jeered at their backs, yelling things that were difficult for Jackson to make out. He turned and looked back at the crack, but it was already too late. If they wanted to mess with him, all they had to do is reach into the crack and yank him out. And it would make him look weak. Jackson clenched his jaw and watched the two men approach. That's when he noticed the street sign at the end of the cul-de-sac.

He was on King Street.

The first of the two to reach him looked eighteen- or nineteen-years-old. Despite the chill in the air, he was dressed in jeans, an oversized Houston Rockets winter coat, and a flat bill cap that featured what looked like a close-up of Andre the Giant's face. He slowed down to eyeball Jackson before turning to his friend.

"Look what the crack gave us this time," he said. They both laughed, but it was hard for Jackson to detect any good humor in it. The way they were looking at him was all menace.

The second man was dressed all in black: black jeans, black letterman jacket with white sleeves, black Jordans. It was an unusual and foreboding choice of attire, but Jackson figured he couldn't really criticize considering his own new look. Besides, both of the men didn't look like the type who would take criticism lightly.

"Have you guys seen a man in a blue sports jacket come through here?" Jackson asked. He figured engaging the young men was his only option at the moment. If he ran, it would take him right past the rest of the group.

"Which sport?" the man in the jersey asked. Jackson realized he must be the leader. The other man was there strictly for action. It wasn't a comforting thought.

"Not that type of sport. Like a nice jacket. Something someone would wear at a fancy dinner."

"Does it look like we have fancy restaurants down here, man?"

The question felt like a trap, so Jackson didn't answer.

"The only person to show up with any type of weird jacket is you. That jacket is an eyesore."

"Don't I know it."

The man turned to his friend in black. "He doesn't look too homeless, does he? There's not enough dirt." He looked at Jackson once more. "You're not homeless."

"No, I'm not." Jackson was surprised that this man had figured it out on his own, but it wasn't as comforting as he thought it would be. There was something in the way the men were looking at him, as if they were testing him.

"So that means you're just a little lost."

"I guess so."

"Good thing we know where you are. I'm Eddie, and this is my friend Miguel."

"Actually, Eddie," Jackson pulled Rose's map out of his pocket and showed it to the men, "I'm just on my way to The Lot. I've heard they can help me out."

Eddie burst out laughing, slapping Miguel on the back. Miguel just stood stoically, looking at Jackson. "The Lot, man?" Eddie said. "That's for homeless weirdoes. And you just told me you're not homeless. Why would you go there?"

"I was robbed last night. That's how I ended up with this coat and nothing else to my name. The Lot seems like the only place to get the help I need."

"How much money did you lose," Eddie asked.

"At least three hundred."

"So you're like some kind of big shot when you're not stranded on my street?"

"Have you heard of GoCoNutty?"

"That expensive coconut water? My girlfriend loves it!"

"That's my product and my company."

Eddie let out a slow whistle. "Man, you *are* far from home. But seriously, what are you doing going to The Lot? It's just a bunch of religious people taking care of homeless dudes. It's not a place for a guy like you."

Jackson couldn't help but feel his chest swell a bit under the heavy layers of the coat.

"You're a self-made man. An important man. You don't need The Lot for help. You need to help yourself."

Eddie's words were like stepping into a hot tub after being in the cold rain. He was right. Jackson needed to do what he was best at, which was taking care of himself.

"Look, Miguel, I made him smile," Eddie said. "I guess he just needed a little encouragement; that's why he stepped through the crack."

"You're a smart guy, Eddie," Jackson said. "In fact, you're the first person I've met who really seems to get what's going on with me today."

"Aw thanks, man." Eddie waved his hand in the air to say no big deal. "So what're you gonna do to help yourself?"

"Huh?"

"See, you're a self-made, important man and all that, and

now you know you gotta help yourself. I'm interested in what you're gonna do seeing as how I'm a self-made man myself."

Eddie was still smiling, but there was a new edge to his words. Jackson started to feel as if the hot tub he was stepping into was actually full of ice.

"I'm in charge of these couple of blocks, so any ways you might help yourself right now fall under my domain. And the way I see it is if you help yourself right here, on my street, it's actually me that's doing the helping."

Jackson tried to keep up with the twisting logic, but was having a hard time focusing. For the first time since he woke up on the sidewalk that morning, fear was coursing through his body, grabbing and squeezing his insides with a vice-like grip.

Eddie took another step toward him, and Miguel took a step to his side, almost as if they were trying to surround him. "What I'm trying to say is that there's actually no way for you to help yourself. You might be a big deal wherever it is you come from, but you stopped being a big deal as soon as you squirted out of that crack. Your only possible chance in this situation is to ask me for help."

"Wh-what?"

"Ask me for help!" Eddie growled, moving his face an inch from Jackson's.

"Hel—Will you help me?" Jackson said, taking a step back.

Eddie laughed, stood up straight, and turned his head toward the man in black. "Hmmm. The big man needs help. There's two outcomes, the way I see it, Miguel. One way is we help this sad sack and he rewards us, since he's the big time."

Jackson nodded vigorously, but Eddie ignored him.

"The problem with that is these rich guys always seem to forget the little people who help them along the way. No, that's no good. That leaves us option two."

Eddie turned back to face Jackson, smiling, but there was nothing kind or jovial about it. It was the smile of a predator who's just cornered his prey. Jackson's legs felt as if they were about to buckle, and he started straining his peripheral vision to find any potential escape routes. He didn't want to hear option two.

"Our second option would be to somehow make sure our big man on campus gives us our just reward *before* he receives any type of help. Let's start with those shoes."

My shoes, Jackson thought with a start. He glanced down, noticing that he was still wearing his Cole Haan wingtips from the night before. They were so comfortable that he had forgotten all about them. He looked back up at Eddie.

"Fork 'em over," Eddie said, beckoning with his hand.

Miguel placed a hand on Eddie's shoulder and finally broke his silence. "Eddie, c'mon. It's cold."

"He'll make it. Guys like him will always be all right. Besides, who knows what else he might have—"

Jackson bolted before Eddie could finish the thought. Both men paused for a moment, seemingly dumbfounded that Jackson would actually try to run, which gave him the head start he was hoping for. To his right was a house with a side yard. Jackson could see through it into the backyard of another house on another block. He shot through the patchwork grass and vaulted over the waist high chain link fence of the new house's backyard. Luckily, his coat didn't catch on the fence, but he hadn't noticed the stagnant puddle of mud on the other side. His feet squelched into its ice cold murk with a squelch, and it felt as if his body temperature instantly dropped ten degrees. Ignoring the sudden shock to his system, he ran through another side yard that put him out onto the next block over.

He could hear the men yelling and cursing behind him. He scanned left and right down the block before crashing forward into a new yard. Dodging a child's bike, he sprinted into a backyard strewn with trash and old lawn furniture, letting the house block the view of his pursuers. He jerked to the left when he noticed the giant shrub that divided this yard from the neighbors. It was the type of shrub he'd had in his own backyard growing up. It took his brain a minute to catch up with his body as he remembered what made the shrub so special.

It was the perfect place to hide.

Jackson dove onto his stomach and rolled under the lower branches, suddenly thankful for the thick skin of his coat. The weak ones snapped and cracked as he pushed his way farther into the covering of the shrub. He prayed that the green of his coat would blend in with the leaves as he maneuvered around on his belly so that he could still see the backyard.

Eddie and three others burst into the yard at top speed. He sucked in a breath and held it, trying to will the pounding of his heart to stop. The three men continued running into the next yard while Eddie stayed, scanning the yard. He started walking directly to his hiding spot. Jackson closed his eyes, jaw clenched, waiting for hands to grab him. After what seemed like an hour, he opened one eye to peek. Two pairs of shoes were moving away from him into the next yard.

He forced himself to count to one thousand as he listened carefully for any sounds of his pursuers. Nothing but the occasional shout from far away. As he counted, he cursed himself for how gullible he'd been to fall into Eddie's trap. He thought he'd already emptied his pockets of all the bad advice he'd been carrying around, but now he knew it wasn't true. The speed with which he'd gone back to believing the lie that he was the big man who could take care of himself was scary. The truth was that he was out of his element and desperately needed help. He reached a hand into one of the coat's inner pockets and imagined grabbing the lie. Slapping it into the dirt with his palm, he flattened it and vowed to leave it in the frozen recesses of that bush.

He ran through his options. He could try knocking on one of the nearby homes, but based on his previous experiences that day, he wasn't so sure he would get any help. He could try to sneak back to the crack and leave the way he came. Or he could just walk down some of the other streets until he was back on a main drag and away from King Street. Really he just wished he could stay in his green, leafy fortress forever, but he knew the men might eventually retrace their steps.

Offering up a prayer for protection, Jackson rolled out of the shrubs. He stood up, quietly brushing off the dirt and twigs. He turned to leave the yard and ran face-first into something that hadn't been there the first time. The object took shape in his mind as a man, someone who'd been waiting patiently just out of sight for him to exit his hiding spot—a man dressed all in black. Miguel.

Jackson nearly fainted as all his blood seemed to drain from his head. He clenched his whole body, bracing himself for whatever violence was about to happen. Instead, Miguel just put a finger to his lips, shushing him. Then he motioned for Jackson to follow as he carefully made his way back through the side yard. Jackson hesitated for a moment, then followed. What other choice did he have?

CHAPTER 6

Miguel led Jackson through a tangled web of side yards, backyards, streets, and sidewalks. Whenever they ventured out into the open, he waited, checking in all directions before rushing Jackson out and forcing him to keep his head down and shoulders hunched. After what seemed like an eternity of ducking and dodging, Miguel led him onto the screened-in porch of an old white two-story home. The paint on the siding was peeling and there was definitely a hornet's nest in the upper corner, but Jackson had never felt so happy to see shelter in his life. As if to add to the surrealism of the whole situation, Miguel ushered him into the house, sat him at a tiny kitchen table, and poured him a glass of lemonade.

"What just happened?" Jackson asked when it became clear that Miguel was a man of few words.

"Sorry about that," Miguel answered. "Eddie is a little crazy. I've known him since we were kids, and he can run a little hot at times. I don't think he really would have done anything, though."

"You could've fooled me!"

"He's just got this short guy complex when it comes

to rich white people. And he smelled it on you right away. I think he just wanted to scare you, but I'm not so sure. It's not every day one of you comes down here looking like he's homeless."

Jackson took a giant gulp from his lemonade. "Yeah, well this is all new for me too. Why'd you help me?"

Miguel was silent for a moment, and Jackson understood he was actually considering the question. "He was taking it too far. I guess I just saw that you really needed some help. Besides, I like the people at The Lot. Eddie doesn't know what he's talking about with them."

"You've been there?"

"My grandpa and I go every once in a while to help out. What, are you surprised?"

Jackson realized he had let his emotions out onto his face once more. "I wouldn't have pegged you for a helper at first glance."

"Well, I wouldn't have pegged you for some rich coconut dude at first glance either."

"So we're even."

They sat at the table, catching their breath and gulping glass after glass of lemonade. Finally, Miguel spoke once more. "Can I ask you something, man?"

"Shoot." Jackson instantly regretted his choice of words, given his situation.

"Why did you think you could help yourself? I mean, if what you're saying is true, there's absolutely *no way* you could help yourself. All you did was egg Eddie on."

Jackson was about to brush off the question. The heat of shame was burning his cheeks. He didn't want to think about what he left back on the ground underneath the bushes. But he owed the young man an honest answer. He had probably saved his life, or at least some unbearable pain.

"I guess it boils down to pride. It's funny because I never really thought of pride as all that bad until today. I think it had always seemed like a strength. But it sure hasn't served me well today."

Miguel nodded. "My grandpa calls that type of thing a 'thorn in the side.' He says I've got one when it comes to appearances. He says everybody has some type of blindspot in their life."

Jackson looked down at Miguel's jet-black Air Jordans. Even though they had been running through the dirt and dust of the street, they still looked pristine. Jackson realized he must have wiped them down when he wasn't looking. He looked down at his own freezing feet. His favorite wingtips were now thickly coated with cold, black mud. He could feel the sludge soaking into the inner soles with determination.

"You should probably take those off, huh?" Miguel asked. "They look like they're totaled."

Miguel left the kitchen and reappeared just as Jackson finished pulling off the sopping shoes and socks. He passed Jackson a fluffy brown towel. "You better wrap your feet," he said. "Otherwise you'll catch pneumonia or something. Don't worry about the mud; it'll wash out."

As he tucked his feet into the soft folds of the towel, Jackson found that he was embarrassed by Miguel's benevolence. Here he was, living in a neighborhood full of feral kids like Eddie, and he didn't hesitate once in bringing him home and giving him a warm towel for his feet. He was probably almost twice Miguel's age, yet couldn't think of a single moment in his life where he had matched the kid's altruism. It all made him feel even more threadbare than before.

"You a fan of Michael?" Miguel asked, breaking Jackson's spiral into guilt.

"Huh?"

"Michael Jordan. Are you a fan?"

"I guess so. I'm pretty sure everyone my age is. But I'm surprised you are. He's been out of the game for a while."

"Well, he's my namesake and all that. I wouldn't say I'm a

huge fan or anything. But parts of his life are really inspiring. He made it big, even though he went through all the grime we live with—his dad's murder—stuff like that."

Jackson vaguely remembered the fact from around the time his Jordan worship was at its peak. "Wasn't that right when he quit."

Miguel lit up. "Yeah, man. You *are* a fan! Have you ever seen that documentary *Jordan Rides the Bus*?"

"I don't think so."

"You have to. It's all about that thorn in your side—pride. It's about how Jordan quit at the top of his game in order to play baseball."

It all started coming back to Jackson—Jordan's humiliating career in baseball. How he went from winning trophies and basking in universal acclaim to playing in the minor leagues to tiny crowds. Jackson remembered the confused derision of the sports press at the time. No one could imagine why he would leave the comfort and joy of being number 1.

"His season started rough," Miguel continued. "He wasn't used to the long hours and thousands of miles the other players put in. He was tough, but he didn't have the experience of all the other guys. He had all that pride in basketball, but it was impossible for him to avoid his weaknesses as a baseball player."

"It sounds awful," Jackson said. "I bet he regretted it right away. I know I would."

"That's your thorn talking, man. Jordan didn't regret it one bit. In the show he says that he had been on a pedestal for so long that he forgot all about the steps it took to get there."

Jackson heard the words like a punch to his gut. Memories of the early days of MadeStrong came flooding back. He remembered the long hours he and Matthew put in. How they would often work late into the night so that their other employees could go home. He remembered all the failed fair-trade coconut plantations they tried out in Thailand, trying to find the perfect flavor. The long, sleepless flights and culture shock. He remembered their first bottle of GoCoNutty and almost crying at how good it tasted. "That's pretty real," he said, "but if I remember it right, that wisdom didn't really help his baseball career out at all."

"It kinda did. It took a year in the minor leagues for Jordan to learn all about that thorn in his side. He saw his weaknesses and became coachable. He listened to his coaches, practiced all the time, asked for feedback, and by the end of that year, his coaches said he had grown a ton."

"Listen, I lived through this. He still wasn't good at baseball."

Miguel laughed. "True. But it made him better at *basketball.*"

"What?"

"When he went back, man. Phil Jackson said that he wasn't all just about his own ability anymore. He wasn't on that pedestal. Instead, he started drawing out the gifts and abilities of his teammates. That year in baseball looked crazy to everyone else, but he used it to remove that thorn. He realized that pride was his blindspot, and he used his baseball career to overcome it. Pride to humility. He led his team to three more consecutive NBA titles." Miguel leaned back and looked at his shoes. "That's why I wear these. To remind me not to go down that path of selfishness. I see it in Eddie and some of my other friends. I want to be that Jordan—his post-baseball return."

Suddenly Miguel shot up from his chair and stuck his foot next to Jackson's. "Tight!" he yelled, running out of the room. Jackson could hear him pound up some stairs and start rummaging around another room. He came back with his arms behind his back and a huge smile. He brought out his arms to show Jackson a pair of used, but still pristine, white high-tops. It took him a moment to realize that Miguel was offering the shoes as a gift. It took another moment to realize that they weren't Jordans.

"Those are Reeboks," Jackson said.

"One of my favorite pairs," Miguel answered proudly.

"But we just spent the last half an hour talking about Jordan!"

Miguel laughed. "Man, I told you, I'm not a *huge* fan. Dude's pretty vain nowadays. I just like that story. And some of the shoes are OK. Nothing beats these Reeboks, though."

"There's no way I could—"

"Humility, man," Miguel interrupted. "It starts with accepting help—and gifts."

Jackson took the shoes from Miguel without another word. As he unwrapped his feet from the towel, Miguel took his mud-crusted wingtips gingerly between a few fingers and chucked them in the trash. Jackson winced and tried not to think of how much he had spent on the shoes. Instead, he focused on slipping his new shoes onto his feet and lacing them up. He stood and bounced a couple of times. "They're super comfortable," he said.

"Duh. They're Reeboks."

"Thanks, Miguel." Jackson was surprised at how much the selfless present was affecting him. It took all his concentration to keep his tear ducts dry.

"No problem. You just gotta make sure you think about that post-baseball Jordan when you wear them. You know, I never asked you your name."

"It's Jackson."

"For real?" Miguel cracked up. "That's funny, man. Like, you're named after Jordan's coach, but I just spent the last hour coaching *you*!"

Jackson broke out laughing, too, until his mind stuck on the word *coach*. He remembered his conversations with Matthew and Rose. He took out his map to The Lot, unfolded it, and showed it to Miguel. "Do you think you can help me get there?"

"That would be no—" Miguel was interrupted by his doorbell. He shushed Jackson and motioned for him to hide behind the refrigerator.

Then he left the kitchen to go answer the front door.

Jackson stared at the side of the ancient refrigerator and tried to swallow the panic that was creeping up his body from the pit of his stomach. *It's nothing,* he tried to convince himself, *just a neighbor or a kid selling candy bars for school.* But he couldn't shake visions of Eddie bursting into the kitchen with his posse and laying waste to his cold, dirty, still-slightly-hung-over body. It would be the perfect end punctuation to the weird story of his day.

To distract himself from the fact that Miguel had been gone for at least five minutes and hadn't offered any type of signal that the coast was clear, Jackson started taking inventory of the explosion of papers stuck to the side of the fridge: bills yet to be paid, a couple drawings by kids who could obviously barely hold crayons, a Bible verse printed on a bookmark, at least three newspaper clippings about The Lot, and in the middle of it all a letter of recommendation for Miguel to attend a local two-year college. Jackson thought of how freely the kid had given him the Reeboks and silently prayed that he was not currently being pounded into oblivion by Eddie and his crew. Jackson couldn't remember the last time he had sincerely prayed so often in such a short time span. Then again, his world was usually full of meetings, numbers, and basking in the praise of others, not hiding in an unknown home from the beating of a lifetime.

The steady drum of approaching footsteps interrupted his thoughts. Jackson scanned the kitchen wildly, looking for anything that might be used in self-defense. He had just settled on a meat tenderizer when a hand reached around the fridge and tugged him into the center of the kitchen.

Jackson's reflexes took over as he broke the handhold on his jacket and unconsciously covered his face. Right before closing his eyes, he caught a glimpse of his assailant. It wasn't Eddie. It took his brain a moment to sort through all the new input—navy blue pants and shirt, yellow patches on the outer shoulders, a radio clipped to the top of the shirt. It was a police officer. And he was not smiling.

"How'd you get in here," he growled. To Jackson, he looked Hispanic and probably in his fifties. The light brown skin of his face was just starting to wrinkle, each ridge a ghost just barely visible. But he still looked as if he could have Jackson on the floor in a submission hold in point two seconds. And his eyes said he was about to.

Before Jackson could respond, the man's eyes found his new Reeboks. "So that's what you're after, huh? You break in here to steal those shoes?" The man's hands started moving toward the taser on his belt.

"Miguel, where the heck are you?" Jackson thought. "No, no," he said, hating the way his voice was shaking, "the guy who lives here gave me these. He let me in."

"I'm the guy who lives here," the man said.

As soon as he said it, Jackson realized the man's picture had been part of the collage on the side of the fridge. Had Miguel been playing him? "I-I'm lost, and these kids started chasing me and this kid named Miguel brought me here to keep me safe and said that these were his shoes and . . ."

Jackson trailed off. The man's face had broken into a grin that widened with every stammered piece of Jackson's story.

"I'm just messing with you, man!" the cop said, slapping Jackson on the back. "Miguel put me up to it."

"Oh man, you looked like you were ready to faint dead," Miguel said, stepping out from behind the cop. "I almost started feeling bad."

"Wh-what's going on?" Jackson asked.

"Jackson, allow me to introduce the grandpa I was telling you about—Grandpa Miles."

"Officer Galvan when I'm on the beat." The policeman offered his hand to Jackson who reached out and shook it despite wanting to scream in frustration.

"I was about to hit you with a meat tenderizer."

"Really now? That would've been a first for me."

"Grandpa Miles's been hit with pretty much everything else," Miguel chimed in. "That's why they call him the sponge around here."

Miles laughed. "I thought it was for how quickly I learn."

"You? Learn? You would be sitting in your squad car on some corner in Five Oaks busting rich people for speeding if you were really that quick. Instead you're busting up dog fights and block parties."

"Someone's gotta do it."

"Ah, you love it and you know it."

"I like a challenge." Miles turned his attention back to Jackson. "Miguel said you're looking to visit The Lot."

"I've heard they're the best place to get help around here," Jackson said.

"Second best to the police, I hope."

"Well, now that you're here . . ." Jackson took a deep breath to start into the whirlwind of his day.

"Now, just hold that in a moment," Miles said, holding up his hand.

Jackson exhaled, realizing he had spoken too soon.

"Grandpa, he's pretty all right," Miguel said. "I think he's on the straight."

"I would hope so if you're inviting him into our home."

"If I wouldn't have, Eddie would have pounded him. He wouldn't have stood a chance."

"Yeah, so I'm still right here," Jackson said.

Miles chuckled. "You are. And I don't mean any disrespect. I just wanted to let you know up front that the most I can do for you is—"

"—take me to The Lot. I get it."

"You've heard it before."

"A couple of times, actually."

"Well, that's good. I was one of the people who first started encouraging people to connect you guys with The Lot."

"You guys? I'm not—"

"I'm sure it's just temporary. Anyways, we've had some pretty good success with cleaning up vagrancy in our community. And we owe it to The Lot. If you don't mind taking the long route, you can tag along with me."

Jackson thought of Eddie and his squad of neighborhood goons and shuddered. "I don't mind the scenic route." He turned to Miguel. "Are you coming with?"

"Nah. I've got some homework to take care of. Besides, you're in good hands."

Jackson was surprised by how disappointed he felt. He realized that in the short hour or so he'd spent with Miguel, he had already started thinking of him as a friend.

"Take good care of those shoes. Don't go jumping in any more puddles," Miguel said. Then, before Jackson could protest, he pulled him into a brief hug. "Keep that thorn in check," he said.

"I will." Jackson stuck his hand into his right side pocket. To Miles and Miguel, it must have looked as if he were getting ready to leave. Jackson opened his fist and dropped the new words into another empty pocket. **Identify and overcome your blindspots**. He wouldn't forget them.

"Off we go," Miles said, leading Jackson into the cold, winter dusk.

Into the wild blue yonder, Jackson thought. He shuddered and tried not to think of what else was waiting for him out in the expanding winter shadows.

CHAPTER 7

Officer Miles and Jackson's first stop was a dilapidated bodega wedged between a laundromat and check-cashing business. They paused outside, and Jackson caught a glimpse of his own reflection in the front window. His face looked worn and disheveled, as if it had been molded by some kindergartner's dirt-covered hands. He imagined walking into a board meeting coat and all, plopping into his favorite leather office chair like the luckiest bum in the world.

And in some ways he was the luckiest. Jackson realized that his journey could be over as soon as they reached The Lot. One day of vagrancy under his belt. It felt like getting hit by a truck. He thought of all the people he had stepped over and ignored on his way between his coffee shop and work. People like Mercy. They didn't have an out like he did. His worst day was their daily life.

"You look like you swallowed something sideways," said Miles, breaking him from his spiraling thoughts.

"Just checking out my new style," Jackson said. "I think it fits."

"Well, I've been checking something out too, and it's not

you." Miles pointed his chin at a display shelf in the window. It was covered in a cornucopia of multicolored glassworks. Jackson's college days had been just wild enough for him to recognize it as drug paraphernalia, a jumble of pipes and bowls painted with pot leaves and the Houston city skyline. "I think I need to have a chat with the proprietor."

"Should I wait out here?" Jackson asked.

"I'm a stickler when it comes to loitering. You better come inside."

They wandered through the aisles of canned goods, energy drinks, and cream-filled pastries until they reached the counter in the back. There were mini displays of postcards featuring Houston landmarks and cityscapes. On either side of the counter were racks of shirts blazing with the logos of the Astros, Rockets, Dynamo, and Texans.

"Manny's a pretty big fan," Miles said when he noticed Jackson's raised eyebrows.

As if on cue, a blocky, bald Hispanic man stepped out of a back room behind the counter. He slowly looked Miles and Jackson up and down and seemed just about to turn around and walk away when Miles said, "Long time, Manny."

"I didn't call you. Why are you here?" Jackson tried not to focus on the raised vein pulsing on the side of Manny's neck. He could probably swallow two Eddies with a little room to spare. Jackson tried to sink further into the folds of his coat.

"Just paying a visit, is all," Miles said. "The neighborhood's been saying lots of good things about your store."

"Really?"

"It's the truth. Mr. Garvey next door told me the teens've left him alone ever since you opened shop. And I used to have to stop by the laundromat at least twice a week because of the muggings. I haven't had to do that in a long time. Probably because everyone's much more afraid of you than they are of me."

Manny laughed, and the muscles in his neck and shoulders rolled and rippled. *Is that a neck tattoo?* Jackson thought.

"Having you here has been real good for the community, Manny. Keep making me look bad, all right?"

"All right, Officer Galvan. You got it. Anything else?"

Miles took out his wallet. "How about a skyline postcard for my friend." He motioned to Jackson. "He needs something to help him remember this day."

"Sure thing. Although he's not looking too good."

"Yeah, well, there aren't many places to spruce up, you know?" Jackson said. They all laughed as Jackson picked a postcard off the display.

"One more thing," Miles said. "Do you think you could clear up your front display a bit? You've got so many good things going on in this store. I would love to see something a little less . . . tacky."

Jackson braced himself to run. But Manny just laughed once more. "Been meaning to do that for ages. It's about time."

Miles and Manny shook hands as Jackson stood in shock. He had to force his legs to start moving once he realized he was about to get left behind in a store owned by a man who could use him for a toothpick.

"I have no idea what just happened," Jackson said as they exited the bodega. "I mean, he was totally hostile when he saw us, and now he's laughing when you call his pipe display tacky. Are you a Jedi?"

"It wasn't *that* Force. Just a little trick I learned from working on *the* force," Miles said. "You can actually boil my job down to motivating people. Sure, we might seem all about controlling through fear or the threat of violence, but 99% of my job is just good, old-fashioned people management."

"You call *that* people management?" Jackson said. "What've *I* been doing then?" He thought of the endless meetings: creative sessions, strategic assessments, hirings, and firings. He had never come close to what he had just witnessed. He had always considered people management to be the regular employees listening to the higher-ups. As in, "I'm the boss, so do what I say." And here was a cop who had every right to pull the cop card, getting his way without even mentioning his inherent power.

"Well, if you're like most people," Miles raised his eyebrows incredulously, "you've probably been doing some people *pushing* while fooling yourself that it's management. It's pretty easy to force someone to do what you want, especially when you're in control, but I've found that it's way more powerful to motivate them instead. See, everyone has something that motivates them. You just have to look and listen closely to figure it out."

"So how about Manny?"

"Really? You didn't see it? You need more help than I thought! It was all over his store. No one has that much Houston merchandise without feeling pride for their city. If he has pride for his city, amplify it by one hundred and you have his pride for his neighborhood. Manny wants to feel as if he belongs."

"Hence the compliments about his presence in the community."

"Exactly. Every word one hundred percent true, by the way. I just wanted to get him in the right frame of mind. I got him thinking about how well he's influencing the community—"

"So when you mentioned the pipes, he could see them the way you do—the negative effects."

"Now you're getting it."

"It's brilliant." Jackson could feel the cold, sharp pricks of jealousy inside of his heart. How could this old cop be better at managing people than a self-made CEO?

"Just part of the job. The fun part," Miles said.

They walked in silence for a while. Jackson's breath puffed out in front of him in fragile clouds. They reminded him of the thought bubbles in a cartoon, except they were all empty.

He was afraid to fill them. He didn't feel ready to admit what he was thinking.

At the corner, they noticed a city sanitation worker sweeping up a growing pile of rancid trash. It looked as if someone had run off with a trash can, strewing its contents in the road as they ran. The worker was sweeping slow enough that most trash had blown away from the pile by the time he added the new bits and pieces. His scowl told Jackson that he probably didn't care all that much. Miles stopped for a moment and exchanged some small talk. The worker looked relieved to have a small break from the foul-smelling chore.

As their conversation wound down, Miles said, "You're doing a great job with all this unpleasantness, Pete. It looks so much better than when I walked by before."

"It's slow going," Pete said.

"Yeah, but you're getting it done. And your boss needs to know." Before Pete or Jackson could protest, Miles had whipped out his cellphone and dialed a number. Apparently he knew the right person to get ahold of because after just fifteen or twenty seconds he was singing Pete's praises to someone whom Jackson assumed was Pete's boss. By the time Miles wrapped up the call, Pete was a Cheshire cat, grinning from ear to ear.

Jackson could still hear the heavy *swish* of Pete's broom when they were a block away. He looked back once and the pile was nearly complete. "More magic," he said, shaking his head.

"Magic would be me getting a couple extra days of vacation. That was just more of my everyday," Miles said.

"So what was Pete's motivation?"

"The same as any cog stuck in the machine of city work. Public recognition. Most of us are used to being told that we need to work harder, faster, better. It's always about the job ahead. So when someone praises us for the job we just did . . . well, you saw it."

"You light up like a thirty-foot Christmas tree."

"I like that. That's one way to put it."

Jackson gulped his jealousy down and decided to try a little humility. He figured he was already stuck in a homeless man's jacket, a teen's shoes, and the body of someone who thought he had it more figured out than he actually did. What could he lose?

"Tell me more about how you learned this stuff," he said. "And no claiming it's natural!"

"I've got to say, you're pretty curious for someone of your . . . current position."

Jackson was through being defensive. It was too exhausting. *Time to roll with the punches*, he thought. "Well, I've got a lot of time to think."

"That's the truth. I guess if you really want to know, people management has always been built into this job. On the average day, I'm going to be outnumbered in most situations. And you saw Manny. Chances are, I'd probably be overpowered too if it came down to it."

"That dude could overpower a pickup truck!"

"No doubt about it. So if I'm going to be outnumbered and overpowered in most interactions, I have to rely on being able to quickly assess a situation and manage it. That's where motivation comes in. I use it to keep the peace. Most people have this TV or movie version of the police in their heads—they think we just use the threat of force or fear of consequence to motivate. And don't get me wrong, some of us do. There is definitely a time and a place for using fear to motivate and manage. The problem is when an officer thinks that's the *only* way to do it. They're the ones who make the rest of us look bad. The ones who are good at this job prefer positive motivations."

"Like a sense of belonging and public recognition?"

"You're getting it. I might have to deputize you at this rate!"

"As long as I can stick my badge on this jacket. I'm starting to like it." Miles laughed at the joke, but Jackson realized there was a bit of truth to it. The day was winding down and the air felt at least ten degrees cooler. Wind was whipping against him, trying to find any little piece of exposed flesh to chill, but the coat pretty much covered him completely. He would almost have called it comfortable, if it wasn't for the smell. He just couldn't get used to the tang of sweat and trash that wafted up into his nostrils every few minutes. "So you prefer positive motivations?" Jackson asked.

"Not always. I started my career trying to keep the peace through fear. I was decent at it, but I didn't really enjoy the job all that much. It took a lot out of me. And our department was set up as a competitive environment. Our bosses used our numbers, promotions, and incentives to motivate us. The problem was that I just couldn't get into the competition. I watched coworker after coworker gain promotions and move on, while I just sat there, working my same beat, growing more and more disgruntled. I started dreading going to work and even questioned my calling to be a cop in the first place. My bosses recognized it, but they just tried to fan the flame of competition, which was like throwing a wet blanket on me."

Jackson was familiar with a competitive environment. He had often used incentives to motivate his employees. But he realized that the same employees tended to win the incentives. He had always assumed it was because they were the best workers, but now he wondered if maybe there were a lot of people like Miles in his office—workers who shut down in the face of competition. "So what changed?"

"Well, it wasn't the environment. Working for a bureaucracy has its perks, but adaptability is not always one of them. What changed was the big, fat envelope that arrived on my desk one morning."

"An envelope full of cash—nice! That would motivate me, too!"

"You've watched too many movies. I'm not on the take.

The envelope was full of letters and drawings from a local elementary school on my beat. I had helped out with an anti-drug campaign by coming and speaking at the school, and each one of the students sent me a handwritten thank-you. As I read through each one, bad spelling and all, it was like a dull flame was suddenly kindled inside of me. I couldn't wait to get out on my beat that day. And you *know* I made that elementary school my first stop."

"So . . . you're motivated by little kid drawings?"

"Not the drawings, man; it's what they represent. I figured out on that day that I'm not motivated by competition or incentives—my drive is a sense of purpose. Those letters reminded me of why I got involved with the job in the first place. I wanted to help people. See, my bosses were boiling the job down to numbers and statistics. But I needed to see the job as people and faces. When I realized that, I went out of my way to start learning the names of the people I met on the job. It changed everything. Competition is definitely a positive way to motivate someone—I've used it myself. But it didn't work on me."

Jackson was reminded of Matthew. He was always interested in going out and meeting the people crazy about GoCoNutty. In their meetings, he would bring in pictures of the people he met, pasting them to the wall to put a face to their numbers. Jackson had always found it a bit dramatic, but he realized that Matthew was probably a lot like Miles. He needed to feel that he was making a difference. That's why he never seemed as impressed with their profits as Jackson. He felt like an idiot.

"My experience in my station taught me something that I use every day," Miles continued. "It's a pitfall to just throw one motivational style over everyone like some all-encompassing blanket. We're all bringing a lifetime of different experiences, thoughts, fears, and dreams into any situation; and we're all going to respond in a different way. That's why I started to pay close attention to the clues all around me about what motivates a person. It's helped me love my job."

"And your job seems to love you back!" Jackson said, thinking of Peter and Manny. He was reminded again of the environment he crafted in MadeStrong. HR was always telling him that their turnover was too high. He had always assumed it was because some people just weren't motivated or bright enough to handle the job. But was that really the case? He tried to think of all the different ways they tended to motivate their employees. He could come up with two: competition and fear. And *he* was the driving force behind those two. It wasn't enough for his employees to just be good at their jobs. He needed an office full of people like Miles. If they *loved* their jobs, the possibilities were endless.

"All right, Master Yoda, it's time for your ultimate test," Jackson said. "What's my motivation?

Miles grinned. "It covers you just as much as that giant coat. But I'm not gonna say."

"Why not?"

"Because believe it or not, motivations can change—just like our hearts. Sometimes we go through life with a heart that's made out of stone, cold to the touch and unmoving. But then something happens that changes us. That stone cracks and splinters, revealing the heart of flesh that was there all along. And when that happens, your whole sense of purpose and motivation changes."

It was like a bell ringing somewhere deep inside of Jackson. *Is that what's been happening,* he thought. He pictured the fissures on his cold heart widening, streaking across it like some new intricate highway.

He looked down at his hands and realized he was still clutching the postcard from Manny's bodega. It was a picture of Houston's skyline in the middle of an idyllic sunset. The silhouettes of the buildings lay flat against the orange and pink backdrop, giving the photograph a warm, hazy glow.

The sun was setting, not just on the postcard, but on some of his core business beliefs. He could no longer manage his people the same way, not if he wanted to craft employees as good at their jobs and as joyful as Officer Miles. He flipped the postcard over and mentally wrote himself a note: **Find out what motivates your employees and use it to manage them.** He stuffed the postcard into another empty pocket. The jacket had become incredibly valuable. Its pockets now carried the wisdom he didn't even know he needed.

"I'll tell you what," Miles said, clapping him on the shoulders. "I want *you* to tell me what motivates you. The next time we meet."

"The next time?" Jackson realized that Miles was pointing at something. He followed his finger to a giant parking lot, empty except for a few vans and people milling about, unloading chairs and setting up folding tables.

"Welcome to The Lot," Miles said.

CHAPTER 8

Jackson gazed out on the scene unfolding before him. A small crew of three or four people in oversized coats like his own were helping unload a slew of scuffed and stained white folding chairs. A few matching folding tables were scattered around the cracked cement of the parking lot. Other than that, there was nothing but knee-high weeds and a cold wind. It looked more like the decaying remnants of a departed circus than the safe haven everyone had built it up to be.

He turned back to Miles and raised his eyebrows. "*This* is The Lot?"

"You were expecting the Emerald City?" Miles chuckled.

"It *has* been a very Oz-like day."

"So which one am I, the coward or the one without a brain?"

I guess that makes me the heartless one, Jackson thought as he turned back to survey Oz, perhaps peeking behind the wizard's curtain. After all the time spent building up The Lot in his mind, he was getting to finally see it was nothing more than a run-down parking lot full of plastic picnic furniture.

"I know it's not much to look at," Miles said, "but wait until the service starts. It'll put those doubts you're feeling in a stranglehold."

"Service?" Jackson asked. In all of his wandering, panhandling, and running from vicious youth, he hadn't really put together that there would be an actual church service at The Lot. He had been so focused on just getting home that he didn't think about the ramifications of the help he would receive.

"It's a powerful thing. Especially if one of you all preach it," Miles said.

"Can't we just get on with figuring out my ride out of here? I want to go home."

"That'll come in time. They handle the logistics of help after the meal and service. C'mon, I'll introduce you to Pastor Mike."

Jackson's stomach gurgled at the mention of a meal, but it was coupled with a jolt of fear at where Miles was leading him. He didn't really want to meet Pastor Mike. Most religious people made him feel uncomfortable. They always reminded Jackson of the impenetrable cliques of high school, seeming to know something he didn't or to speak a language he didn't understand. They acted as if they were so put-together and perfect. He tried to avoid them as much as possible.

They walked through the growing crowd of people unloading chairs. Jackson noticed that it wasn't just vagrants in huge coats—now there were suburbanites in the mix. He couldn't help but rabidly soak in their designer labels and shiny smiles. These were his tribe. It kindled the fire in his heart for home while at the same time reminding him of just how exhausted and broken he felt. He considered offering to pay one of the men to trade clothes with him before realizing that the whole reason he was there in the first place was that he didn't have any money.

Miles strode through the crowds and stopped before a tall,

skinny man dressed in jeans and a flannel shirt. He had the beard and horn-rimmed glasses of the type of urban hipster Jackson would often see in Montrose or The Heights. Jackson pegged him as a sound guy or a musician of some sort, but then Miles was speaking to him.

"Pastor Mike, allow me to introduce you to Jackson. My grandson helped him out a little today."

This is Pastor Mike? Jackson thought as he shook the man's hand. *He has a beard!*

"It's nice to meet you, Jackson," the man said. "Don't worry, it's not a stage name. I really am a pastor."

Jackson realized that he had been wearing his shock on his face once more. "Sorry, it's just that—"

"—it would be easier if I were in a suit and tie. I get it. We're all dealing with stereotypes of some kind. The pastor, the cop, and the homeless guy."

Jackson didn't even try to correct him or tell his story. He knew he would just be stopped and told to wait until some elusive later date. Besides, he had to admit he was a little intrigued by the bohemian pastor. At least he didn't feel uncomfortable. Yet.

A new group of three dirty men in ill-fitting clothing interrupted them by stepping directly in front of Pastor Mike.

"Ahhh, the three Petes!" Pastor Mike exclaimed. "Welcome back! I'm putting you on chair locking duty. You remember how they click together?"

The three Petes exchanged a glance that was either "Duh!" or "Uhhh?" It was hard for Jackson to tell through the gristle and grime of their faces. They shuffled off toward the rapidly growing lines of folding chairs.

Pastor Mike returned his attention to Jackson. "You want to help out? We could use you."

Jackson could have leapt into the air. It was the first time the entire day that someone had asked for his help. He had grown so used to feeling lesser-than that he hadn't even imagined there might be a task for him in all the hustle and bustle of the setup.

"I would love to," he said.

"I'm going to leave you to it, then," Miles said. "I'm sure I can round up a few more people before services begin. I'll find you in a bit."

Pastor Mike led Jackson to an old brown van that actually blended into the surroundings perfectly. He pulled open the back door to reveal even more folding chairs. Reaching in, he began to pass them to Jackson in pairs.

"Are you sure you're going to need this many?" Jackson asked.

"We've been running out the last couple of times, so I brought some extra. Have you ever been here before?"

"No." They started moving with their loads of chairs toward the nearest incomplete row. Jackson saw one of the Petes moving down the row, clicking something into place in the middle of the chairs.

"Well, great!" Pastor Mike said. "First times are always exciting."

Except this one is in the midst of a freaking tornado of firsts! Jackson thought.

Soon they fell into a rhythm of unloading and unfolding the chairs. It felt good just to work, to actually be useful for once in his day. Jackson was relieved that Pastor Mike never tried to preach at him or get all religious. Instead, he just let Jackson work. Every once in a while someone would come up to greet him. It was always high-fives, handshakes, or hugs. Jackson couldn't believe that Pastor Mike could genuinely *enjoy* so many people. He watched his face closely for any cracks in the friendliness, but the man's smile just grew deeper with every interaction. He seemed like the real deal.

Occasionally, Jackson noticed that Pastor Mike would pause in his chair work to reach down the middle and fiddle around with something. Eventually there would be a "snap," and he would resume working on unfolding chairs. On the fourth or fifth time, Jackson's curiosity got the best of him, and he decided to break his rhythm.

"Why do you keep doing that?" Jackson asked.

Pastor Mike looked up from where he was currently jiggling something between the chairs. "It's the lock. If you don't lock the chairs together correctly, they all just shift and scrape, which gets a little distracting when all of these are filled."

Jackson looked down the row to see one of the Petes reaching down between the chairs. "Didn't you hand off the job to those three guys earlier?"

Pastor Mike nodded. "Yep. Just looks like they're missing a couple every once in a while."

"Wouldn't it be more efficient to have them do something else while you take care of the chair locking? That way you wouldn't have to spend all that time checking their work."

"You're concerned with my efficiency?" Pastor Mike looked at Jackson as if he had suddenly sprouted a third arm. "That's a new one."

"It's just . . . something I think about, I guess. In all my free time." Jackson considered telling the whole story. The moment seemed right, but he was suddenly enjoying the anonymity of his oversized jacket. He could see Pastor Mike was observant and genuine, which meant he was also the type to ask questions that could drill right down into your heart. The less he knew about Jackson's day, the better.

"Interesting." Pastor Mike did not seem convinced. "To be honest, Jackson, I think about it more than I let on. I mean, have you *seen* how many of these chairs I've had to re-lock?" As if on cue, he reached between two more chairs and a few seconds later there was a *snap*.

"Let me tell you about why I let men like the three Petes do what they're doing, even when it might seem inefficient. It all traces back to when I first got involved with this ministry. Do you know much about church business?" Pastor Mike asked.

Jackson shook his head.

"Well, it's actually a lot like real business. There are budgets, projections, growth models—anything and everything you could think of to help a ministry be more efficient. So I took over The Lot from its previous minister and stepped into a mess of confusing and conflicting systems and procedures. You following me so far?"

Perfectly! Jackson wanted to belt out. He knew the challenges present in taking over someone else's business. He could imagine Pastor Mike buried underneath a deluge of e-mails, demands, and impossible expectations. But he didn't want to give away too much, so instead he just shrugged his shoulders.

"The only thing I could think to do was contain it all in my own hands, since then I would know everything that was happening. Soon I was completely running the show. The Lot stopped being confusing and haphazard because I was micromanaging every decision. Instead, it became overwhelming. I was killing myself to get every service off the ground. I would work so hard in preparation each week that by the time the actual event rolled around, I dreaded coming down here. I would have nothing left to give my volunteers or our attendees. I could tell no one was all that happy, so I just started trying to micromanage even more. I figured if I could so clearly identify the problem, I would also be able to figure out a solution."

It all made sense to Jackson. He had a similar approach at MadeStrong. He had crafted the flow of work so that most decisions crossed his desk, no matter how small. He figured he was the main driver of success behind the company. It was branded with *his* name, after all.

"That's when I met The Grizz," Pastor Mike continued.

"The what?"

"Not a what—a who. The Grizz was one of the old guard here at The Lot. He had been coming since long before I took over. I had heard some tall tales about him—he was an old Vietnam vet who was a true philosopher and thinker. But in all my frantic running around each weekend, I had never met him. Then, one night as I was trying to redraw a map of chair and table placement, a man with a beard down to his belly button sauntered up."

"The Grizz."

"Exactly. He proceeded to introduce himself before launching into a series of deep theological questions that I hadn't tangled with since seminary. I mean, this guy could have been a professor the way he was interrogating me about matters of faith. I couldn't get anything done. We only completed half the setup before it was time for me to deliver my message. But when I approached the microphone, my head was swimming with The Grizz's questions, and I couldn't focus for the life of me. The worst part was I felt like The Grizz was leaving with none of his heartfelt questions resolved. It was a total disaster."

Jackson took a moment to look around. Seats were quickly filling up with a mixture of suburbanites, young artists covered in tattoos, and vagrants. To his surprise, everyone was smiling and talking with one another. It was hard to imagine The Lot he was looking at ever being a disaster.

"That week, I did the only thing I knew to do. I called up an old mentor, one of my professors in seminary who had led an inner-city ministry for his entire career. I didn't want to call him. In fact, part of my decision to manage everything myself came from a desire I had to impress him with a successful first ministry. Instead, we met over coffee so I could explain the mess and learn from the best. He listened carefully to all of my complaints with everything and then said: 'Show me your plan.' I began telling him all of my plans for the ministry and what I wanted The Lot to become. He interrupted after a couple of minutes and said, 'I didn't ask you to *tell* me your plan, I said *show* it to me. I want to see it.' I sheepishly had to admit that I didn't really have my plan in writing."

"But you had your vision and different processes in place, right?" Jackson asked. "That's usually enough."

"That's what I thought, too. Like, I *knew* I needed a plan in place and had all the intentions of writing it down, but I just didn't have the time, tools, or resources. My mentor explained to me that a written plan brings structure. And structure is what everyone craves. It's like the skeleton of the building. You can't put art on the walls without something to keep those walls upright. Right there in the coffee shop, we sketched out a rough plan of action for my ministry, complete with large goals and smaller, personal goals. It was as if a giant weight just fell off my shoulders. But my mentor wasn't done. He started using the one word that always made me think of a teacher looking over your shoulder as you work: *accountability*."

"I hate that word!" Jackson said. "Give me autonomy or give me death!"

"Right? My mentor explained that it wasn't the 'I gotcha!' type of accountability. He mentioned a group of small business owners who met together for lunch every couple of weeks to discuss their plans and goals. It's hard to argue over great burgers and maybe a beer, so I thought I'd give it a shot. I was hooked from that first time. We essentially just start with successes before talking about where we are stuck or stalled in our plan. There's some creative problem solving, a whole bunch of encouragement, and—most importantly—the feedback I needed to stick with my plan."

Jackson tried to imagine the lunches. He was used to talking about his success; it was a surefire way to establish a pecking order in any social situation. But talking about problems? To a bunch of guys over *burgers*? It sounded terrible. Still, it was hard to argue with the success of Pastor Mike's ministry. The evidence was surrounding him, piling up every minute. Every smiling face, every person helping set up, reminded Jackson of the dismal workplace he had almost single-handedly created.

"What about The Grizz?" he asked, hoping to change the subject.

"It's funny," Pastor Mike continued, "I actually ended up putting what I learned to good use with The Grizz. The week after the coffee meeting, I wrote down a whole plan for The Lot and forwarded it to all my volunteers. When we met down here that Friday, people were actually eager to get to work. It was confirmation that assigning jobs based on my own vague ideas and whims was actually pretty demoralizing. My volunteers wanted some structure, and I gave it to them. So when The Grizz sidled up to me, I decided to give him some structure too."

"You put him to work?"

"He didn't even have a chance to get one question out. I put him on chair duty, pretty much doing what we are right now, and the man thrived. I think I even heard him humming some Zeppelin as he worked. Now, he didn't necessarily complete the work the way I would have—you probably would have called it inefficient. But The Grizz was happy to help out. He even started escorting some of his friends to the 'best seats in the house.' It was a small task, but he took pride in it."

Pride. The word jabbed at Jackson's heart like an angry hornet. He had always considered his own confidence to be an integral part of his success. How could he be a successful CEO without an overreaching belief in himself? But it wasn't just about him. He was running a business. And when he conjured up the faces that passed by him daily, he didn't see pride. Instead, it was as if the scales fell from his eyes and he could see the emotions and motivations that he'd always just passed by. Determination. Grit. Maybe a little disappointment. But he couldn't for the life of him imagine one face full of pride for their job. Maybe Matthew, but Jackson wasn't ready to go down that rabbit hole.

Instead he imagined being back in his office with the door shut. A blank piece of paper was sitting on the desk in front of him. Next to it sat his favorite Montblanc pen. All he had to do was pick it up and put down his plan.

He was aware of something else in the room. It wasn't a person—it was more like a nebulous idea floating somewhere above his desk. He closed his eyes, not caring if Pastor Mike thought he was crazy. He needed to grab that thought. His business, his employees, his future—everything depended on it. The insight fell over his shoulders like a tattered, extra large coat, uncomfortable yet absolutely necessary.

He needed help.

One of the Petes bumped into Jackson, jostling him out of his reverie. The Pete reached between the chairs and clicked them together. "Gotta double check a couple of these," he grunted as he passed.

"A man with a purpose," Jackson noticed.

"You're a quick one, Jackson," Pastor Mike said, "Which means I have a *special* task for you."

Jackson knew that Pastor Mike was a man of God—it was part of his name after all—but he swore he detected a glint of something a little devilish in his eyes. He followed the bearded leader through the large crowd that had officially stopped working, and started milling during their conversation. Jackson could smell the tang of chicken soup in the air and momentarily thought of ditching the pastor for the food. But he was pretty sure there was some story in the Bible with similar circumstances that ended in lightning strikes, so instead he followed right on his boot heels.

As they walked, Jackson reached down and opened one of the side pockets on his jacket. He thought of Pastor Mike's story and the wisdom it contained. He plucked the lesson from out of the story—**Write down your plan because structure fulfills purpose**—and dropped it into the pocket. Although what he really needed was a cell phone and some cash,

Jackson started to think maybe his new jacket wasn't so trashy after all.

They stopped before a different van full of speakers, wires, and other electrical equipment. Everything was tangled like Christmas lights in an attic. "Time for you to have a little purpose of your own," Pastor Mike said, clapping Jackson on the back.

Jackson just stared at the mess as he tried to wrap his mind around the gargantuan task. He turned to protest, but Pastor Mike had already disappeared into the crowd, leaving him alone with the cornucopia of electrical equipment.

The wires twisted over each other to spill out of the van as Jackson lifted out one piece of the equipment. It was obviously some type of sound system; he could tell that much from the microphone mixed in with the rest of the equipment. He looked around The Lot and saw what he figured was the stage. The small area was already lit with some portable lights. He could hear the hum of a generator mixing with the voices in the crowd.

"Well, it must not be *that* hard if he's giving it to me," Jackson said out loud. The thought wasn't as calming as he'd hoped.

He managed to drag all the components to the staging area piece-by-piece. That wasn't so bad. He was actually pretty good at untangling, and nothing was really all that heavy. But next came the hooking up. He looked through the van twice but couldn't find any instructions.

Visions of power outages and electrocutions danced through his mind. As the sun went down, the cool night air actually made the idea of a little extra electricity somewhat tempting. Jackson just couldn't deal with the possibility of his friends and family finding his crispy remains dressed in a ridiculous jacket surrounded by a homeless congregation.

That's when he resolved to do something that the old Jackson of twenty-four hours ago would have slapped him across the face for even considering. But Jackson was starting to think that old version may have been a little bit of a delusional jerk.

He walked into the crowd determined to put his crazy new Jackson plan into action.

He was going to ask for help.

CHAPTER 9

People were avoiding him. Of that Jackson was certain. And it had nothing to do with the fact that he looked homeless. For the first time that day, he was part of the majority. So it came as a surprise when he couldn't find anyone who would make eye contact with him, let alone help him wire together a potentially life-ending piece of electrical equipment.

Jackson made his way up and down a few of the rows of chairs in his search for a friendly face. Most of the seats were filled. Some of the more weathered people already had their heads back and were snoring loudly. There weren't many people left standing, and the ones who were seemed to be trying their hardest to look busy. He couldn't figure it out. He had just been toiling away in front of the group, trying not to be electrocuted. It should have been obvious by now that he needed some assistance.

"Oh," Jackson thought as he stopped his progress through the rows, "that's it." It *was* obvious that he needed some help, which was why everyone was avoiding him. Pastor Mike had stuck him with the job no one else wanted. Probably because the last person had been zapped into oblivion!

As Jackson started feeling frustrated about his situation, he caught the steady gaze of a man who seemed interested in his plight. But instead of relief, Jackson felt like turning and running from the entire event. He *knew* the man.

It was Walt Ashley, the angel investor who was behind many of the recent successful Houston-area startups. Although they had never met, Jackson looked up to him as their social and work spheres seemed to complement one another. At one time he had even toyed with the idea of getting Walt involved with NightHawk. It all led to two important thoughts that sliced their way into Jackson's brain:

1. *What in the world is he doing here?*
2. *Please let there be an earthquake, right here, right now.*

The ground didn't shake. It didn't even tremble. Instead, Walt held up his hand and made a "come here" gesture. Jackson started walking the other way, but he noticed Walt following him out of the corner of his eye. He decided to just walk back to the electronics—hoping that Walt was as wary of the towering mountain of wattage as everyone else.

He reached his task and picked up two random cords that he was pretty sure weren't plugged in. Jackson tried to look confident as he shuffled over to another piece of equipment that looked as if it had holes that could fit the cords. Footsteps approached. He considered just jamming the cords in and ending it all right there. Then he felt a tap on his shoulder.

Bracing himself, Jackson turned around. Walt was smiling in a pretty genuine way that didn't really fit with the gruff, all-business genius Jackson had heard about. Jackson kept his eyes cast downwards. For the first time that day he actually prayed there was enough dirt and grime on his face to distort his features. *Let me look homeless*, he chanted in his mind. *Please let me look homeless.*

"Looks like Pastor Mike put you on Rubik's duty," Walt said, sticking out his hand. "I'm Walt Ashley."

As much as he wanted to, Jackson couldn't leave the hand in the air. The years of business sense embedded in his DNA made it so that no offered hand could go unshaken. He grabbed the outstretched hand and said, "Nice to meet you."

Walt waited for him to keep speaking, but there was no way Jackson was going to tell him his name. It seemed as if the coat, dirt, and stress were all working together to obscure who he was, and he didn't want to mess that up. He just needed to change the subject. "Why did you call it Rubik's duty?" he asked.

"One of our volunteers compared it to a Rubik's cube. Everyone else who ever tried it agreed, so the name stuck."

"I guess it's a better name than what I've come up with."

"Oh. And what's that?"

"The bomb squad."

Walt stopped and seemed to look him over once more. Jackson wondered if he'd said too much. "That's pretty good," Walt said. "It *is* kind of like all those bomb defusing scenes in movies. 'Don't cut the green wire, just the red!' I work around marketers quite a bit, so I know quick thinking when I hear it."

Jackson needed to change the subject—fast. "You sound like you've done this before."

"Only every week. I think Pastor Mike has some weird, sadistic experiment going on where he likes to give people the job and see how long they make it before asking for help. Thankfully no one's knocked out the power grid for downtown Houston—yet."

Despite all the pressure to hide his identity, Jackson felt a tinge of relief that Walt actually knew what to do. "Please, take over," he said.

"I could use another set of hands," Walt replied. "We can get it up and running in no time."

Since Walt was familiar with the equipment, Jackson

assumed he would dive right in. Instead, he pulled out his cellphone and started poking at the screen. "I guess we're not in a rush?" Jackson asked after a minute or two.

Walt laughed. "Don't worry, I'm not texting or looking up cat videos. I'm looking at the schematic I sketched out for all of the hookups."

"Haven't you done this a hundred times?"

"Probably more like two hundred. But I look at this every time. I figure the extra time and attention is well spent, especially when the alternative is turning into a piece of extra crispy KFC."

Jackson's stomach gurgled, which was a little disturbing, so he was thankful when Walt started giving him instructions in how to hook up the sound system to the generator. They soon fell into a rhythm: Walt supervising and instructing while Jackson worked plugging everything in. Every once in awhile they were interrupted by a homeless person who would stop by to greet Walt with a hug or a handshake. Everyone seemed to know him, and Jackson noticed that he seemed more and more energized by every greeting and small chat. He found himself imagining if he were in Walt's shoes. The old Jackson would have no time for people like that, especially if he had a task in hand that needed his attention. But the new Jackson— the one dressed in an ill-fitting coat who had survived on the cold streets of Houston for an entire day—he wasn't sure. He thought that maybe he would have a new response. Maybe he would be as energized as Walt.

"NOT THAT WIRE!" Walt shouted, breaking him from his reverie. Jackson immediately dropped the cord he was holding and jumped back. A tiny shriek exploded from his throat. As he scrambled backwards, bracing himself for an explosion, he realized that Walt was still calmly standing in the same place. And he was smiling.

"Not cool," Jackson said.

"You're the one who made the whole bomb squad connection. I just wanted it to feel like the movies."

Jackson walked back and picked up the final cord. He thought of his shriek and started giggling. It was hard to stay mad at someone who just made you feel like you were in the final scene of your own action movie. "I hope you don't mess with any of your startups like that," Jackson said.

Oh, crap. In all the adrenaline, he had let his guard down. Walt hadn't mentioned what type of business he conducted. A homeless person wasn't supposed to know something like that!

"You know who I am?" Walt asked.

Don't panic! Act normal! Make something up! "Somebody pointed you out earlier. I didn't really know what a startup was, so they explained it to me."

He chanced a glance up from the electronics. Walt was squinting at him, as if he were trying to see through him. "Should we try it out?" Jackson asked, hoping to escape the scrutiny.

"What? Oh . . . yeah. Hit that red switch over there."

Jackson flipped the switch and an ear-piercing squeal rocketed out of the speakers. The gathering winced and covered their ears.

"Turn it off! Turn it off!" Walt shouted, but by then Jackson had already flipped the switch back down.

"I think your schematic might need some adjusting," Jackson said. He had never appreciated such an excruciating noise before, but at that moment he wished he could lean forward and kiss the speakers without his lips burning off.

"It's not the schematic," Walt explained. "We just have the microphone placed too close to the speakers. Move it over there, Squeaks."

Jackson placed the microphone where Walt was motioning. "Squeaks?"

"Well, you never told me your name." Walt waited. Jackson

did too. "So since you're not being too forthcoming, I decided to call you Squeaks. I think it's fitting based on that noise you made a few minutes ago coupled with the horrible squeal you just subjected us to."

"I guess it's a better nickname than Squeals."

"That's the spirit! Now try it out."

Jackson flipped the switch tentatively, ready to shut it all back down. This time there was nothing but a little electronic hum coming from the speakers. Walt motioned for him to tap the microphone. Jackson tapped, relishing the moment. He had always wondered what it would be like to be a rock star. Tapping the mic and listening to the corresponding thud from the speakers seemed like a good first step.

"All right, Squeaks," Walt said, "let's go see if the coffee's warmed up yet."

As soon as they left the makeshift stage, a young man with an acoustic guitar stepped out of the audience. They made their way to a table behind the rows of chairs as the man started strumming some folky chords on his guitar. He actually sounded pretty decent. Jackson was expecting an electric piano and some old school hymns. This guy's song about God sounded more like an old Bob Dylan or Neil Young song.

They reached an old percolator, and Walt poured him a steaming cup. The cold air was sharp against Jackson's exposed cheeks, and he appreciated the way the coffee seemed to spread warmth down into his chest as he swallowed it. The sun was quickly descending, leaving the old lights of the parking lot to light the scene. Jackson took another sip. He felt peaceful.

"This is exactly why I love coming down here," Walt said, swallowing from his own Styrofoam cup.

"How long have you helped out?"

"I am actually one of the founders. So I guess it's been at least five years."

Jackson couldn't believe that *the* Walt Ashley had helped

lay the foundation for a homeless church that meets in an abandoned parking lot. "I'm surprised you have the time," Jackson said. "I mean, because it sounds like you've got a pretty important job."

"I guess you could say that. But part of why I love my job and work so hard at it is that it enables me to do something like this. These nights are what recharge me and remind me of why I keep throwing myself into my job week-in, week-out. Besides, these guys need me."

"To set up that death trap."

Walt laughed. "Partly. But I'm also the financial backer. Pastor Mike wouldn't be able to keep it going on the donations of his church."

Jackson just about spit his coffee into the night air. "You're financially backing this?" he asked, forgetting for a moment that he was currently a benefactor of Walt's philanthropy. "There's no return on your investment!"

"I *knew* it!" Walt said. "You've got more business experience than you're letting on. So how is that?"

"From a past life," Jackson answered. It was meant to be a brush off, but the words resonated with him and he knew they were true.

"You're just full of surprises, Squeaks. And as for a return on my investment, I guess you're right, in a sense. It all just has to do with how you think about money."

"Money is money. If you're making your money back, it's a sound investment. I don't see how else you could think of it."

"I like to think of it as a blanket."

Jackson about dropped his coffee cup. Here was Walt Ashley, one of the most successful investors in the area, comparing the lifeblood of business to a blanket. He marveled at how one day could keep plunging the depths of the bizarre, sending him deeper and deeper into the rabbit's hole of the weird. "A blanket," he said, trying to sound as neutral as he could in the circumstances.

"Not the most poetic image, I know. But hear me out. Money can be our big, woolen blanket. We engulf ourselves in its folds, and it makes us feel warm and safe. It seemingly protects us from all the elements outside. I see this in some of the startups I meet with. They're all wrapped up in their revenue, showing me pie chart after pie chart of how much money they've made in a short period of time. They are all nice and cozy, smiling from inside the cocoon of money."

"Sounds nice," Jackson said. All the mentions of warmth and comfort had him wishing for his own woolen blanket to fight the dropping temperatures. He imagined meeting with Walt on his own terms. How different it would be if he could show up in a perfectly tailored suit to lay out MadeStrong's success. He figured his company had a pretty comfortable blanket of money he could demonstrate to Walt.

"Doesn't it? But here's the thing: imagine that you're all wrapped up in that woolen blanket on a sinking ship. Suddenly all that warmth and comfort is just a façade. As soon as that wool hits water, it's going to drag you to the bottom of the ocean."

"That's a little morbid."

"Good. It should be. The way so many people are looking at money *is* morbid. You see, those startups that show me all their revenue; they nearly always break down when it comes to profit. The excuses usually start when I ask to see what their expenses are and measure it against their revenue. There's lots of talk of the future at that point, and the rationalization of expenses, but actual profit usually is a good sign of how a business is doing. I stay away from the business leaders who think they are successful but are not actually making any real money. They might have an enormous amount of revenue every month, but I can see that they are sinking slowly in their woolen blanket, refusing to push it aside."

Jackson thought of his own blanket—the one he would present to Walt. He remembered Matthew's fears about their numbers the night before and how he had brushed him aside. Was he tangled in a blanket? He realized he wouldn't want to show Walt his expenses. The excuses popped into his head immediately: "We're launching a new product, so expenses are temporarily high. They'll even out once the product is successful." He heard himself through Walt's ears and knew he was on his way to the bottom of the ocean. NightHawk was going to sink him.

"Are you OK?" Walt asked. "You're getting kind of pale."

"It's the caffeine," Jackson lied.

"Since I work with startups, it can be especially tricky. In those cases, a business could actually be making a lot of profit but still be in a dangerous situation. Growth burns cash faster than a fire in a gunpowder factory. It usually requires additional investment, and it is very easy for new expenses to exceed the growth that's happening. If a business isn't meticulously tracking their expenses and capital outlay in order to make sure they are still generating a profit in the midst of growth, things can get out of control. That's why I've got to look at the business leaders carefully. Are they all wrapped up in the blanket of money? Or are they seeing it for what it is— something useful that you need to be careful around."

I'm wrapped up! Jackson wanted to say. He just wanted to admit it to someone—that he had made a mistake. He wished for his cell phone so that he could call Matthew. He needed to tell him he was right.

"So that's the way I think about money," Walt continued. "I know it's a bit eccentric, but it's helped me over the years."

"You could call it the 'false sense of security blanket,'" Jackson said.

"That's perfect, Squeaks! You sure you're not an undercover marketer?"

"In my day job, maybe. So how do you keep a good perspective with all the money you're handling?"

"Now *that's* a good question. I wish more of the startups I meet with would ask those types of questions. And the answer is pretty simple. You need to know your numbers inside and out. It's not enough to have them in your head. They need to be written down, and you need to look at them. All the time. Not just quarterly or monthly. All. The. Time. It's just like setting up that sound system. I've done it hundreds of times, but I still consult the schematic beforehand. I might *think* I know something, but it's better when I *know* I know it. I've met too many business leaders who *think* they know their numbers, only to end up bankrupt. It always seems to come out of nowhere, but when we dig into their numbers, we find that bankruptcy was embedded in them right from the start. They were wrapped up in the false sense of a security blanket."

Jackson tried to fight down the panic he felt surging into his fingertips. He needed to call Matthew and really look at their plan. He needed to know if NightHawk would sink them. He hoped it wasn't too late. "It all sounds pretty dangerous," he said, trying to keep the conversation going as he worked out a plan.

"For entrepreneurs it is. But it wasn't until I was ten years into my career that I learned the real danger. It took someone outside of my business to help me see the light. In fact, I probably would be one of the sinkers if it wasn't for my business coach. I was just as wrapped up as everyone else, except that my numbers were actually really good."

"So what's the danger?"

"I figured that as long as my numbers were good and I was making a profit, life was OK. I was so tied up in my business that I failed to see how every other facet of my life was falling apart. I was making good money, so life had to be great. Then my coach started asking me questions about life outside of my business. Things got pretty awkward. I grew pretty upset and defensive. He just listened to me rant. When I was done, he asked me the most important question anyone's ever asked me: 'What do you want to be remembered for?'"

As soon as he said it, Jackson felt the question burrowing its way deep down into his heart. He could practically feel all the advice vibrating in the pockets of his jacket. It was as if the whole day had been a siege on the walls of his heart, attacking every belief he had planted as protection. And now cracks were forming in the walls. Every belief, philosophy, and source of pride was tumbling, and in the midst of the chaos, the simple question had broken through to him. *What do you want to be remembered for?* He felt as if he were out of breath.

"The question was a real gut punch," Walt continued. "It really irked me. I ended up storming out of the coaching session. But the thought stuck with me. I started to look for answers and realized that the way I was running my business was all about my business. If I died right then, I would be known as a deceased investor in startups. My board would replace me, and the business would keep moving forward. And that would be it. I went back to my coach the next week humbled and shaken. He helped me remember some of my old drives and passions—the reasons I started my own business in the first place. I had been sacrificing myself at the altar of profit—and for what? To make more money. We set about forging a new plan, this time something that considered life holistically, not just business. That question was the driving force. I had to figure out what I wanted to be known for; then I had to figure out what type of business would allow for that to happen in my life. I realized that the whole point of making money with my business was to free up time. And it wasn't for idle recreation. It was time that I could use for what I'm really passionate about."

Jackson remembered the look on Walt's face every time someone stopped to chat him up. He really was alive in the midst of The Lot. The joy he saw in Walt's smile was something he wanted in his own life, something he didn't even know was missing until that day.

"You see, Squeaks, I'm not successful because of how much

money I make. I'm successful because I can sponsor The Lot. My real success is measured by every one of those seats that's filled and every cup of coffee that's poured tonight. I get to give back in ways that ignite my heart and soul."

"I want that too," Jackson said without thinking. Everything Walt was telling him was rekindling something inside of him. It was like suddenly realizing he'd been living with hunger pangs without knowing what to call them.

He unsnapped the left-hand pocket—one of two main compartments on the jacket. It was deep and the button was smooth, as if it had been opened and closed thousands of times during its lifetime. Jackson imagined all of the change that had been collected in that pocket. But also the insults. The cold nights. The pain, shame, and heartache. He wanted to put something special in that pocket—something full of hope. **Know your numbers, inside and out**. It was a key piece of advice that he knew MadeStrong would pivot on. He snapped the pocket closed. Only one pocket left.

Jackson realized that Walt had turned to face the makeshift stage. His admission had been buried underneath a swelling applause as the young guitarist finished his songs and Pastor Mike took the stage. He was going through a standard greeting and saying something about a special guest speaker. Jackson was finding it hard to focus on the words since everything felt so mixed up and raw inside of him. He was about to just confess everything to Walt when another surge of clapping filled The Lot. The guest speaker clambered out of the audience and onto the stage. It took Jackson's brain a moment to catch up with his mouth that was now involuntarily hanging open. He recognized the deep Navy hue of the man's Brooks Brothers sport coat. It was *his* jacket.

The man who robbed him slowly took the stage and approached the microphone.

CHAPTER 10

When Jackson was nine-years-old, he had his first (and only) physical altercation. Tommy Finkle stole his *Return of the Jedi* Boba Fett action figure on the playground and refused to return it. Helplessness mixed with a seething rage inside of Jackson as he jumped to try to grab the figure that Tommy was dangling over his head. Finally, in what his peers would later call a "killer move," Jackson kicked Tommy as hard as he could in the gut. He plucked the toy from his hands as Tommy doubled over in gasping pain. The young Jackson paused to consider how easy it was to be violent. *Maybe this is the quickest way to get what I want*, he thought. But in that moment, Tommy fully recovered and tackled him to the ground. Any future aspirations toward using physical violence were pummeled out of him that day by Tommy Finkle's abnormally large fists. And Jackson left them there, mixed in with a bit of his blood on the playground wood chips.

At least, he *thought* he had left them behind. As the homeless man shuffled to the microphone in *his* jacket—the man who had single-handedly destroyed the straw walls of confidence Jackson had so carefully erected around his life—a familiar feeling of pure and absolute rage started filling Jackson from the tips of his frozen toes. He figured if he started beating the man, he could get a solid five or six punches and kicks in before the shocked audience would pull him off. He certainly wouldn't get in too much trouble for it, especially when everyone found out the whole story.

Jackson clenched his fists and bent his knees. Just as he was about to bum-rush the stage (he wondered if someone in his position had invented the phrase), Walt stepped in front of him and put a hand on each of his shoulders.

"I don't know what the deal is, but you're not going up to that stage," he said quietly.

"You're right; you *don't* know," Jackson spit back. "So let go of me. This is *my* business."

"Technically, this whole night is kind of my business. And I say you hear him out, Squeaks."

"And if I don't?"

"I don't think it will end well for you." Walt jerked his head back toward the stage.

Jackson took in the homeless man once more. He realized it was the first time actually seeing him. The night before, he was more an extension of the city. In Jackson's mind he was interchangeable with any other homeless person huddled up on the sidewalk and asking for change. That afternoon he had been too busy chasing after him to take in what he looked like. He was more just chasing his own sport coat.

Now that he could see the man in detail, he understood what Walt was trying to tell him. The man could give him a pounding that would make Tommy Finkle shake with jealousy. He was tall and lean, and Jackson could tell that he wouldn't have been able to button the front of the sports jacket if he'd wanted to. His shoulders were square and boxy, giving him the profile of a retired athlete or boxer. Still, Jackson would have the element of surprise.

"That guy's a thief!" Jackson hissed at Walt.

Walt's eyes widened and the corners of his mouth turned down. "Terrence?"

"You *know* him?"

"Pretty well, actually. At least, I thought I did. He's been doing all right for a while now." Walt hesitated.

"Yeah, he's all right at *stealing from me!*"

Jackson turned toward the stage and was about to move forward when Walt grabbed his arm again. "Just hear him out, Squeaks." There was something in the way he said it, as if he was desperate for it to all be a mistake, that made Jackson pause.

At the front, Terrence cleared his throat and began to speak. "First of all, big thanks to Pastor Mike for letting me testify tonight. I want you all to listen close because I have a word for you. And I'm not saying that from up high—I'm the lowest of the low, and most of you all know that. But I've been shown something, and now I've got to bear witness."

Funny, Jackson thought, *I'm about to bear witness, too, as soon as this . . . whatever this is ends.*

"It's cold out, huh," Terrence asked the audience, blowing into his hands for emphasis. "Don't think I've ever been this cold at this time in the year. I woke up yesterday morning feeling the cold aching in my bones. And I was just sick of it, you know? Sick of waking up covered in cardboard. Sick of fighting with myself every day. Sick of feeling so cold. I spent all yesterday shivering on the sidewalk, people just stepping over me like another piece of trash, no one looking in my face or even noticing how hard I was fighting to stay clean. I've won the fight against heroin every day for the last five years, but do they even see that? No way. Those people, they look at me and see someone who's losing, you know? There was one guy in fancy clothes who I asked a dollar from so I could get a coffee. He looked at me, right in the face, and didn't even *see* me. He told me I was just getting in the way. After that I figured, what's the point? If everyone already thinks I'm the loser, why do I need to win another day? At least heroin makes me forget the cold."

There were a few gasps in the audience. Jackson raised his eyebrows at Walt. *See?* he mouthed. Walt frowned and pointed back at the stage.

"I got off the wall last night and went out looking to score. It was like this huge weight just flushed out of me. But I didn't feel good. I just felt empty. Who I was, everything I stood for, seemed to be draining out of me. I had a picture of this parking lot and all of you, but I shook it out of my head. I wasn't ever coming back, you know? I was ready to just give my life away to heroin. But as I stood there and just tried to empty myself of all the good things I've learned here the last couple of years, I noticed this weird lump right in front of me. It was a person. And not just *any* person. It was the guy in the fancy clothes, just passed out in the gutter right there in front of me—in the middle of the night!"

That was me! Jackson wanted to shout, but something inside was stopping him. A tiny, thin voice seemed to be whispering *What if you're wrong?* And it was true. He had been wrong to verbally abuse this guy, just as he had been wrong about so much already that day. But that still didn't give him the right! This guy had stolen everything from him—he was wearing the evidence!

"I'm not gonna lie. In my state, I was ready to roll him right then and there."

"That'd teach him!" someone shouted from the audience.

"No, no! You see, I realized that *wouldn't* teach him. He'd wake up only to realize he'd been taken advantage of by a no-good junkie. Where's the lesson in that? He'd go through life still thinking of people like us as *nothing.* And in my case, he'd be right."

Jackson's mind was reeling. Where was this all going? The man was talking as if he *didn't* do exactly what Jackson knew he did.

"So I bet at this point you're wondering about this," Terrence continued. He held the lapels of Jackson's sport coat out and let go. "As I looked down at the guy, all I could think about was how helpless he seemed. And it was brutally cold. He was going to freeze, or at least get sick. So I tried to wake him, but the guy was out of it. I couldn't get much of a response out of him. I was standing there, looking at the man whose words had cut me deep, and this new thing filled me up. It wasn't the need for a fix anymore. I guess Pastor Mike would call it compassion. I remembered something he taught here a year ago. It was about Jesus telling us to turn the other cheek—to forgive our enemies. When I first heard it, I thought it was crazy. You can't live on the streets and just turn the other cheek when someone lashes out at you. But looking down at that passed-out dude whose words had hurt me, I think I finally got it. Jesus wasn't just talking about how we *need* to forgive. It wasn't some Bible class checklist rule. He was talking about how we *can* forgive. See, he already forgave me for my years of drug use and all those dark things I've done to serve that addiction. And if *he* could forgive *me*, then I could forgive that man."

What the heck? Jackson thought.

"But it wasn't just about the idea of forgiveness. In that same passage that Pastor Mike taught us, Jesus said if someone takes your coat, give them your shirt as well. Put your money where your mouth is. I had on my big coat, and I was thinking about how much warmer it was than that guy's fancy jacket, so before I knew what I was doing, I just traded it with him. I wrapped him up as tightly as I could, and I didn't feel anger or anything for him. Just worry. I put this skinny little thing on," Terrence pulled at the jacket once more, "and instantly started to freeze my butt off. I had to go find that vent on 5th and huddle over it all night. But as my teeth clattered and clacked, that little needling voice telling me I had to use was gone. Not just quiet. Gone."

Terrence paused and wiped at his eyes with the sleeve of Jackson's jacket. "I realized something last night. Pastor Mike is always telling us that we matter. It's the rest of the world that doesn't always seem to think so. But last night, when I was feeling the lowest of the low, I had an opportunity to help someone. That's how God works. He puts us on a collision course with brokenness every day and helps us be his agents of healing. That man needed me, and I was there. It doesn't matter what our lot in life is. What matters is our heart."

And with those words, Jackson's heart broke. Terrence's words were the final blow. He had built his view of the world on judgment and misconception—his own tower of Babel. In his pride, he failed to see things as they truly were. He lived out the assumption that he was better than the people around him, and here was a homeless man who had selflessly shown more compassion, grace, and forgiveness in one moment than Jackson could even comprehend. *Oh God,* Jackson thought as his world finally fell apart. *Oh God, oh God, oh God.*

Terrence cleared his throat, and when he spoke again, the shakiness was gone. "I know Walt is out there somewhere. He's always told me that a life without vision is a blank birthday card—it looks like a birthday card, but it's missing the most important part—the message. I never really knew what he meant. I'm sure some of you are with me in that boat. Tonight I want to say that I finally get it. Like, my life has been the blank birthday card. I look just like a lot of you, but I've been missing my heart. I've just been trying to survive instead of really living. But when I gave that man my coat and made him comfortable, everything became clear. In helping him, I found my heart."

"Preach it, Terrence," someone shouted from the audience.

Jackson just wanted him to stop. Every word was like a sharp, stabbing pain. He could feel the false comfort of his old life floating away, and the thought of the unknown future seemed a little scary.

"I know what I need to do now," Terrence said. "I need to help people. I've wasted too much time fighting for myself. Now I need to fight for others. And that fancy man showed me the way. I'm gonna start collecting coats for the people down here. *Free* coats."

Clapping burst out from the front of the audience. Soon a roaring cheer rocketed through the rows of chairs. Terrence blinked.

"So start spreading the word. Anyone you know that has a coat they don't need, tell them to get in touch with Pastor Mike or me. No one's gonna be cold down here this winter. You hear that, Walt?"

Jackson looked over to see tears pouring down Walt's cheeks. He gave two thumbs up to the stage as Terrence smiled.

"I found my vision!" Terrence said.

"Along with a new wallet!" a gruff voice shouted from the audience.

The Lot went silent. *He's right*, Jackson thought. His stomach sank, and he realized he was actually rooting for Terrence. But that didn't change the fact that his wallet and cell phone were gone.

"I'm no lying junkie, man. Not anymore," Terrence said. "I knew that man was gonna need all of that when he came to. So I emptied his pockets and wrote him a little note. Told him he could find me here. Then I put everything in the pockets of my coat right where he could find them."

Jackson slowly reached into the main right-hand pocket of the jacket—the last one. It was deeper than he had originally thought. He dug his hand down into its depths until his fingers hit something. It was a piece of paper. Underneath, he felt his wallet and his phone.

In normal circumstances, Jackson would have cussed for at least five minutes and looked for the nearest person to blame. But nothing about that day had been normal. Instead, a giggle burst from his throat. Walt looked at him sideways, but

Jackson no longer cared. Let him look. His wallet and phone had been there the whole time.

The Lot erupted in applause. Pastor Mike joined Terrence on stage and gave him an enormous hug. Jackson watched in shock, his hands still jammed in his pockets, feeling his wallet, phone, and note.

"Terrence's note is in there, isn't it," Walt asked. "You're the guy he was talking about."

Jackson found that his voice wasn't working yet. All he could do was nod slowly.

"I *knew* you weren't homeless!"

"How?" Jackson managed to croak out.

"I've been doing this for years. It has to do with the eyes and the stories they tell. Most people here, they have this special kind of light in their eyes. It's always flickering, like it could be extinguished at any moment. But not you."

"Not me," Jackson said. For the first time that day, his difference from the people surrounding him brought no joy. He thought of the blank birthday card Terrence was talking about. He wasn't even that. No pictures of balloons or streamers or anything celebratory. He was more like an ornate tomb—beautiful on the outside but dead and rotting on the inside.

"So what's your name, Squeaks," Walt asked.

"Jackson."

Walt doubled over with laughter. Jackson had always wondered what it looked like to "guffaw." That night, as homeless people and volunteers shifted in their chairs to check out all the commotion, Walt showed him his first guffaw.

"OK, so I've run through every possible joke associated with my name," Jackson said once Walt finally managed to get control of himself, "and none of them are *that* funny."

"You're Jackson Strong," Walt said in a shaky voice, and it looked like he might explode into another fit of laughter.

"Wh-what?"

"Jackson Strong of MadeStrong. Purveyor of GoCoNutty. I've seen you at a luncheon or two. *That's* why you kept looking so familiar to me!"

Jackson looked down at his coat, his dirt-streaked pants, and his new Reeboks. "Guilty as charged," he said, which just sent Walt into a whole new round of laughter.

"This is a story I have to hear," Walt said after calming down a second time.

Jackson was finally able to tell his side of the story from start to finish. There were a couple of places where he wanted to fudge some of the details in order to save face, but he didn't. He figured what better time to start putting some humility into practice than right there with Walt.

When he was done, Walt let out a long whistle. "You've been on a journey," he said.

"Everything and everyone just kept pointing the way here. And now with Terrence . . ." Jackson trailed off.

"Let me tell you a thing or two about Terrence," Walt said, and Jackson was thankful he didn't have to try to put it all into words. He was worried the lump in his throat would betray him.

"I first met Terrence a few years ago. The guy didn't have a lick of belief in himself, but I recognized a fire that I liked. He'd been sober a couple years at that point, and I knew that doesn't come without a pretty fierce daily battle. So I decided to start coaching him a bit here and there, usually as we were setting up and taking down The Lot. But Terrence had the same limiting belief as a lot of the guys I've tried to encourage over the years. He thought leadership was some innate quality that you're born with—you've got it or you don't. So I started attacking that belief bit by bit. Leadership isn't some personality trait; you have to work at it. And most of the work is reflection and vision. I started asking Terrence some questions and listened to him reflect. I could see he was starting to think differently about his life and himself, I mean, he remembered that whole birthday card analogy, right! Well, one day a couple of months ago, I asked what I call 'the kicker.' The reflection of all reflections."

Jackson grimaced. He didn't want to know, but then again he desperately did. He just wasn't sure his heart could take much more.

"I asked Terrence, 'What do you want your life to look like three years from now?' He started avoiding me after that. Guess it was a pretty powerful question."

Walt looked up, and Jackson followed his gaze. Terrence and Pastor Mike were making their way through the crowd.

"Most of the people I deal with in business are pretty dominant," Walt continued. "And dominant people have the most blindspots. It's tough for them to be a great leader because everyone else can see those blindspots, but in their own minds they're perfect."

"That was me," Jackson said without thinking. It was him. He imagined the MadeStrong offices. He was no longer walking through the offices as if he were the king in his jungle. Instead, he was the laughing stock—the guy annoying everyone with his arrogance and obliviousness. He could see Matthew gently trying to reach him and make him aware, always with respect and care.

"The best leaders are the ones humble enough to face their own blindspots," Walt said. "They know just what everyone else knows. Everyone's on the same page. And there's great communication."

Terrence and Pastor Mike were only a few rows away. Terrence looked up and locked eyes with Jackson. Jackson's heart froze as Terrence stopped in his tracks. They stood like statues, staring across the divides that had always separated them. Then Jackson reached up and grabbed the collar of his ill-fitting (but warm) coat. He flipped up the collar as if he were popping the collar of his favorite Burberry jacket. Then he gave Terrence a thumbs-up.

A wide grin stretched across Terrence's face as he continued to make his way to where they stood.

"I think I can finally see," Jackson said to Walt.

"Then it's time for me to ask the question," Walt said. Terrence and Pastor Mike finally reached them, and before Jackson could protest, Terrence had pulled him into a giant bear hug.

"The question?" Jackson asked, his voice muffled by his own sports jacket.

"What's your life going to look like in three years?"

EPILOGUE

3 Years Later

Jackson fiddled with the cufflinks on his Burberry sports jacket. They were a gift, a customized set of sterling silver Cartiers whose backs were engraved with a single word: *Grit*. He tried not to imagine the conversation going on behind the heavy oak door in front of him. The board of MadeStrong had been in heated conversations for the last three weeks over the new division Jackson and Matthew had proposed.

As if on cue, Matthew sidled up beside him, a stack of folders and papers under one arm. "They're still going at it?"

"Like teenage stepsisters."

"Well, you can't blame them. You did throw out quite the curveball."

Jackson grinned. It *had* been the perfect pitch. To everyone else, it seemed to come out of nowhere. A new clothing line from a company known for their coconut-infused beverages? But when Jackson had been standing in that freezing parking lot three years ago, he had decided to choose a new path. He figured such moments of absolute clarity only unite our heads and our hearts a few times in life, so he had to follow its lead, no matter how strange or incongruent it appeared to be.

That's not to say that there hadn't been doubts. Jackson had adopted Matthew's business coach Vince as his own, and he lived up to his reputation by asking some tough questions. Normally a clothing line would be a risky venture, but the MadeStrong spin convinced Vince it just might work.

Matthew shuffled through his papers and pulled out their joint business proposal. "Your vision is a pretty compelling read," he said as he passed the proposal into Jackson's hand, "but I have to say that my budget is just a *little* bit sexier."

At that moment the doors swung open and Robert Franklin, head of the board, motioned for Jackson to step inside. Matthew turned to leave, but Jackson put a hand on his arm. "This has as much of you in it as me. There's no way you can't be here for this." He turned toward the board. "As I'm sure you already read in this fine document, this is my strange idea. But it's *his* brilliant work."

The board stared at both men as the door swung shut behind them. Jackson stole a glance at Matthew who turned pale and looked as if he might throw up. Robert cleared his throat.

"So this is the plan?"

"Yes, sir." Jackson felt a familiar defiance rising from the pit of his stomach. It was *his* company. Who were they to— he pushed the thought back down. That was the old Jackson. The one in check. On timeout. "We've already decided that we won't even try to move forward without unanimous approval."

"Unanimous?" Robert chuckled. "Jackson, you realize we couldn't even unanimously agree on the definition of the word *unanimous*?"

"Still, I think it's a good plan." He patted Matthew's shoulder and watched him gulp in surprise. "Matthew's done incredible work. This would be the shift I think we need, and I want everyone on board. Otherwise it's not worth it."

As soon as he said the words, he felt they tasted true. He hadn't ever realized that truth had a taste—not until he started seeing his business coach and meeting up with Walt every couple of weeks. The questions they asked were the kind that stung like wasp stings. It hadn't been easy. He'd even had a couple of dark patches when he thought about quitting, giving up and letting the selfish Jackson off his leash. It usually took only a day or two before he either put his foot in his mouth or managed to singlehandedly cause some minor workplace disaster. After a few rough patches, Jackson decided it was time to give his old, arrogant self to the pound.

Still, it was exhausting to continually be faced with his own flaws and follies. At first, he answered with half-truths or by shifting the blame onto anyone he could think of, but the words almost seemed to rot on his tongue. When Jackson finally started answering with the truth though, there was no bad aftertaste. Instead he felt refreshed. Free. He'd developed a taste for the truth.

"You'll drop it if we don't agree? All that work?" Robert asked.

Jackson pictured the proud faces of his employees from their meeting that morning. He had worked hard to make sure everyone involved understood his vision and their place in it. For the first time he had encouraged their own ideas and creativity, allowing their passion and excitement to change his initial vision. And they were proud—every single one. He couldn't imagine telling them the bad news, but he had a feeling they would make it through. In fact, he was confident it was something they could weather together. "We will."

"Well, it's an awkward position to put yourself in. Quite different from the Jackson of old." Some of the board members nodded in agreement. Jackson steeled himself for the bad news he could tell was coming. "Good thing we like this new Jackson. And we especially like the solid financial plan of your partner in crime."

Matthew turned to Jackson in shock.

"We?" Jackson said.

"Unanimously."

The relief that flooded through Jackson was three years in the making.

"Understand that we still have questions. But your numbers look good, and the altruistic social good thing is very of-the-moment. We think it will work."

Jackson floated through the rest of the conversation two feet off the ground. He couldn't focus on the details because of the anticipation he felt. The unanimous approval was a definite success, but what he *really* wanted to do was tell his staff. After the obligatory salutations and handshakes, Jackson and Matthew left the meeting room and headed back downstairs to Jackson's office.

Matthew still seemed a bit tongue-tied as they paused outside Jackson's door. "Did that really just happen?" he asked.

"Sure did. Guess they thought your numbers were pretty sexy as well."

"But—you—I was actually *there.*"

Jackson felt a pang that he could now call by name: remorse. "Listen, Matthew. You should have been there for every meeting. Truth is, even though the company shares my last name, you're the one who's made it what it is." He thought of some of his early conversations with Vince. "I can see now how I was more an obstacle than an advocate in the beginning. But not anymore. I want you to be there, bringing your number sense, managerial know-how, and weird sense of humor. The board needs to know you."

The look on Matthew's face made Jackson realize he should have said those words a long time ago. "Quit looking at me like I just dropped an armload of adorable puppies on you. We've got a staff meeting to attend."

That seemed to snap Matthew out of it. "Where *is* the staff?" They both looked around at the empty office floor.

Jackson grinned. "At the meeting. Put on your jacket; we're late."

＊　＊　＊

The back room of El Presidente Tapas y Vino was pretty much how Jackson remembered it, only this time he had made the reservations in advance. His staff were already seated around the long, Brazilian mahogany table, drinking wine and enjoying tapas. In the past, all conversation would have stopped the moment Jackson walked in. Now his employees turned and smiled, and he smiled back, letting them know they should just keep enjoying the moment. Speeches could come later.

The head of the table had been left empty. Jackson walked toward it but stopped when he realized Matthew wasn't following and was about to take an empty seat near where they walked in.

"Matthew, get over here," Jackson said.

Matthew gave him a quizzical eyebrow raise, but joined him at the head of the table.

"This one's yours." Jackson pulled out the seat and practically pushed Matthew down into it by the shoulders.

"Umm, shouldn't you be the one sitting here."

The old Jackson would have agreed. Instead, the new one said, "You know, Jesus said you should never take the best seat in the house for yourself. When we take the best seat, the host could tell us that we're in too good a spot and make us move to a lower seat in front of everyone. Instead, we should pick a more humble spot. Then there's always a chance the host will tell us to take a better seat."

"I-I'm honored," Matthew said.

"The way I see it; we tend to naturally think a little too highly of ourselves. That means we're always going to think we deserve something a little bit better than what we actually do. It's better to be seated by someone who knows you well.

And I know you, Matthew. You've never stepped on anyone in order to get ahead. Which is why you deserve this seat more than anyone else."

"To be honest, I thought about stepping on you a couple of times."

Jackson laughed. "You and everyone else in this room!" He walked back to Matthew's old spot and settled in.

The conversation flowed around the room, engulfing Jackson, mixing with the scent of wine and grilled meat. He looked around the table at the excited faces and reflected on each of their individual involvement in the project. But it wasn't just their effort that impressed Jackson, it was knowing where each of them was coming from. He knew their strengths and weaknesses, when to count on them and when to delegate to someone else, when to admonish, encourage, ask questions, inspire. He knew them as more than just employees. He knew them as *people*—hope-filled, contradictory, creative, communal *people*.

It was no longer his jungle when he looked over the room. It was exactly what it looked like, a giant table. Everyone had a place. No one was left out. And he wasn't some god-like king. He was just another member—one with a few more responsibilities—but a member nonetheless. At one point the thought would have made him feel like a failure, but the last three years had taught him it was actually linked to his success. Because he was a human being too, full of brilliance *and* flaws. It was still funny to him that the most humiliating day of his life led to true greatness.

Jackson stood up and the room quieted with the help of a few friendly shushes. "I used to always begin speeches like this by saying, 'My fellow Americans.'" A couple people chuckled at the memory. "But that wouldn't be appropriate these days. Sure, it's true, we *are* fellow countrymen, but that's not how I would define the people in this room. You're here not because you're good at your job; you're here because you're *excellent*.

Matthew, me, this company—we wouldn't be anything without you. So this meal isn't so much a celebration as it is a way for us to say 'Thanks.'"

The room filled with applause and clinking glasses.

"MadeStrong is about to take a giant leap forward. It will be a totally new market for us, but we're confident in the plan. After all, there's a little bit of each of you in it—how could it go wrong?

I also wanted to share some news." Jackson paused to look at Matthew. He wondered how he would take it. He couldn't help but leave him out of the loop one last time, for all the right reasons. "We've decided to give the new division its own name. Somehow continuing to brand things with my own last name felt a little . . . weird. So I'm proud to announce that the clothing line will be branded with what I think of when I think of my good friend and partner Matthew. Allow me to introduce you to True Grit."

This time Matthew was clapping just as loudly as everyone else. "Thank you," he mouthed, and Jackson tipped his glass of water before taking a swig.

*   *   *

Outside the air slapped against Jackson's exposed cheeks, stinging him with the sharp edges of a Houston December. He blew in his palms and rubbed them together, remembering that fateful day when just getting warm seemed impossible.

"It's pretty cold," said a voice approaching him from the side. "I may need to treat you to a coffee."

Jackson turned to find Terrence grinning at him. The streetlight illuminated his neatly trimmed facial hair, the speckles of gray giving him the air of a college professor. It was hard to believe this was the man who had been splayed out across the sidewalk asking for change just three years ago.

Jackson's eyes were drawn to the bundle Terrence was

holding out to him. Some faded fake fur peeked out from the tattered olive green. Jackson grabbed the jacket and slid it over his sport coat. Instantly, the bite of the air melted away.

"Where'd you find this old thing," he asked, trying not to give away the tears in his eyes.

"Been holding onto it for a night just like this," Terrence said.

"You heard the good news?"

"Walt told me. I got over here right away. The donation center can run for a couple of hours without me. Might even run better."

By now Jackson was used to Terrence's self-deprecating humor. He knew that what it hid was an incredible talent that managed to create one of Houston's fastest-growing non-profits from the ground up. Because of him, there wasn't a soul in Houston that would go cold that evening. They'd all be wearing the proper winter attire, some of them even dressed in Jackson's old designer threads.

"Can you believe it, Terrence? They loved it!"

"I believed it from the start. You'd have a heart colder than this night if you didn't love it."

"Are you prepared for an influx of donations?" It was Jackson's favorite part of True Grit—in fact, it was the whole reason for True Grit in the first place. Every piece of clothing would be branded with a picture of the jacket he held. Each tag would tell the story of one of the homeless people Terrence's non-profit was helping, and for every piece of clothing bought, they would donate one to Terrence. It seemed crazy, but Matthew had done the math and made it work.

"Are you kidding me? You've seen The Lot recently. The demand always seems to outweigh the supply. Bring it on!"

Terrence stuck out his hand and Jackson took it, feeling the cracks and creases and knowing the hard years they represented. They shook and talked about some of the finer details.

As Jackson watched Terrence walk down the block, back toward his donation center and food truck soup kitchen, he zipped himself up in the old, musty jacket. He unsnapped each pocket and remembered the advice he'd stuffed in them that day:

Don't be afraid to think differently and ask for help.

Work less so you can live more.

Identify and overcome your blind spots.

Find out what motivates your employees and use it to manage them.

Write down your plan because structure fulfills purpose.

Know your numbers, inside and out.

Project what your life will look like in three years

The truth was that the pockets were empty. The lessons he learned that day filled up his life instead. He thought back on that morning three years ago when he woke up in its folds, cheek pressed into the fur of the hood. To any passerby, he probably looked like one of the lost, someone at the absolute bottom.

But now he knew how wrong they would have been. His bottom had been the night before—the proud, celebratory dinner. That morning had truly been his awakening. And the olive jacket wasn't the tattered old rag everyone saw as they passed. It was his shell—his cocoon.

And he had emerged a new creation.

THE SEVEN PRINCIPLES OF ENTREBUSINESS

Recently, I was in a coaching session with a local small business owner. At EntreResults, we like to begin our sessions with a series of questions meant to help us understand the individual background, education, experience, and desires of our clients. One of the driving principles of our company is to speak the truth, no matter what, and having as much background information as possible helps us achieve that goal. The business owner answered each question directly with the confidence of someone who is used to making a myriad of decisions every day. Then I said this:

> "I want you to think of someone in the business community you consider to be a great leader. Someone you know personally. What makes them a great leader?"

The man hesitated, then looked at me like a deer caught in the headlights. Every answer up to that point had been quick and calculated. Now he stammered, clearly wracking his brains. He talked around the question for a couple of minutes—thinking out loud about what makes a great leader and listing celebrity leaders: authors, coaches, successful billionaires—all before circling back to the original question of someone he knows personally. He looked at me with a furrowed brow, clearly thinking what I've thought so many times in my career:

It shouldn't be that hard to think of a great leader I know, should it?

The reality is that most of us would struggle to answer this question. We can usually think of coaches, politicians, ministers, or humanitarians that embody true leadership, but it suddenly grows complicated when we narrow the focus to the world of small businesses. Most of us could probably list some "OK" or "good" leaders that we know, but when it comes to "great," we're suddenly as stumped as a freshman holding a boutonnière on prom night.

I've found that many people I work with, whether they're solopreneurs, own a 50-person company, or lead a division of 10-15 people, don't consider themselves great leaders.

It's a bit strange, especially considering the vast library of resources on leadership. There are many great books on the subject, including profiles of some tremendous business leaders. However, most revolve around famous big business leaders or humanitarians. While these are great examples, it can be a struggle to find connections to small businesses. That is why my focus is on how to be a terrific leader in the small business community. By developing excellent leadership abilities in the realm of small business, you may one day advance to be a leader in the middle-to-large business community.

This is Jackson's story. He perceives himself to be a successful *businessman*, but the reality is he is a failing *leader*. His view of leadership is a misconception we deal with often at EntreResults: Leadership is something you're born with. Either you're a great leader, or you're not.

While this may be a useful line in the sand for those who already feel comfortable as leaders, it's a limiting belief for everyone else. And, in our experience, it's simply not true.

Leadership is not only a character trait—it's a skill. Great leaders are developed, not born. That is why we begin our workshops with the question. We want to combat any existing expectations that we hold some magic formula that will instantly make everyone in the room successful. We want our clients to know that they are not Jack—there are no magic beans.

We are coaches, and as such it is our job to motivate, impart wisdom and strategy, and act as a form of accountability. That leaves the nitty gritty work of change and growth to our clients. There's no way to instantly become the great leader that eludes many of us. But with focused work, reflection, and guidance—it is entirely possible.

Many small business owners and managers expect that crafting leadership begins in the workplace, among the hundreds of decisions, challenges, and interactions that occur daily. But true leadership begins with you. In order for your business to change, *you* must change.

The lessons that Jackson learns about being a business leader are carefully selected from the vast array of wisdom, knowledge, and experience found at EntreResults. We want to clearly present you, the reader, with the common blind spots, misconceptions, and pitfalls facing many small business owners. Through Jackson, we want you to experience the hard work of truly becoming a great leader.

Each piece of business advice that Jackson learns along the way is grounded in reflection and humility. There is no way for us to clearly see our own blind spots if we are not willing to allow people to speak into our lives—often pointing out the messy spots we would rather avoid. Humility is part of what we do at EntreResults. It is what leads people to see clearly.

Each of the principles found in this book are meant to work together. It would not be enough for Jackson to hold just one of them in his pocket at a time—he was meant to carry them all, allowing them to mix inside the pockets of the jacket, forming new connections, melding together in interesting ways—ultimately becoming a new inner network of wisdom undergirding every decision Jackson makes in the future.

The principles are also not short-term patches. Each business point is essential for long-term growth and success. One of the core beliefs of EntreResults is that we practice what we preach. We want to share these principles with the world because they are the same principles we want to improve in ourselves.

We understand that undergoing deep personal change can often be a journey as arduous as Jackson's. Though you may not find yourself stranded in downtown Houston, chances are this book has led you to pause and reconsider the way you think about your business. Take a few minutes to reflect on the key "pockets" of wisdom Jackson learns throughout the book.

1. Don't be afraid to think differently and ask for help.

As business owners and leaders, most of us naturally think differently in the way we see the world. It was probably this mindset that led us into starting our own business or into pursuing leadership. We understand we can push through so-called boundaries and that there is always a solution to problems that seem impossible to solve. However, this kind of different thinking is not the kind of thinking I'm talking about in this point. I'm talking about thinking differently about what our businesses need to reach the next level, and the kind of help we need to seek. But a couple of obstacles prevent us from reaching out for help. One obstacle is that we naturally tend to be stubborn, and sometimes even prideful. It's usually not in our nature to ask for help because we feel like we should be able to figure it out ourselves, or we feel like no one could possibly tell us how to improve our businesses.

Another obstacle is that many business owners are fearful of what outside help might expose. We want to improve, but it's too painful to have faults and deficiencies exposed in our businesses. We know we need to change, and we know we need help, but our confidence level is too low to ask for help.

Personally, my bent is to lean more toward pride and thinking I should be able to do everything myself. It's easy to think, "It's my business, I started it, and I know what's best for it. No one else would be able to understand." However, what we have to understand is that learning to ask for help is *vital* to moving our businesses forward.

I'm talking specifically about the help that can be derived from outside business coaches and advisors, although this concept also applies to asking for help within the business. Asking for help significantly shortens the time it takes to grow the business from point A to point B, and it also reduces risk.

One day, Allen,[1] a gray-haired man in the mortgage industry, reluctantly came to us to ask for help. He had found us while looking at the internet, and after our first meeting admitted he had not wanted to ask for help. He figured he should be able to succeed on his own without help, but when truly facing reality about himself, he could see that seeking assistance was one of his weaknesses. He then described his past business that had failed several years before. Although many factors had caused the business to fail and declare bankruptcy, Allen realized that one cause was his tendency to

---

1   Note: All of the examples in this section are based on real situations from our experiences over the years but are not real people.

make decisions quickly and abruptly. He also made decisions with emotions and knew he needed guidance implementing more logic and planning.

A coach on our team helped him develop two solutions:

1. They put together a one-page plan for his business, beginning with guiding principles and core values of Allen's business. Then, they articulated the three-year, one-year, and quarterly financial metrics for his business and established key performance indicators. They also created goals based on hitting these financial targets while living within the company's guiding principles and core values.

2. Second, they developed meeting rhythm schedules that allowed for decisions to be made in coordination with other key people, including outside advisors. This prevented rash decisions being made based on emotions.

Allen currently has a growing business and sleeps better at night knowing he is doing everything within reason to prevent the failures that occurred with his other business in the past. But he first had to step back and think differently about himself and his business. He had to realize he needed to reach out for help.

2. Work less so you can live more.

One of the most common problems I see with the small business community is the natural inclination to constantly work. Sure, when the business starts, owners dream of taking time off, long vacations, and extreme flexibility—all of the things they couldn't get with a normal career. They work like crazy at the beginning, knowing hard work is what it takes to get a business going. As a result, their entire model depends on their daily input. Fast forward to the future: they have a decent income but are stuck in the day-to-day grind.

We were referred to Jenny, the owner of a videography company, because she was working all of the time. In fact, the first time one of our coaches met her, it was hard to even get her to concentrate on the initial strategy sessions. She was obsessed with answering phone calls and texts throughout the introductory coaching session. Jenny wanted help and knew she needed it, but didn't know how she would even have time to meet with us.

We worked with her to develop this plan:

1. We spent the first three months focusing all of our attention on freeing up Jenny's time. Jenny delegated some of her financial data entry and hired an assistant to help her with other admin duties. She also ended up firing a time-intensive client who had been sucking up her time, energy, and joy. This client wasn't profitable and was costing Jenny far too much of her resources. After three months, Jenny was able to take three-day weekends with her family.

2. In the next phase we worked with Jenny on her hiring, training, and delegation processes within the company. We increased the prices for her services, decreased the collection time from customers, and then used that extra cash flow to hire an office manager who was also good at phone sales. This completely changed Jenny's life.

She now continues to work, but focuses on the area of business she enjoys. Because she did the work to strategize her schedule and responsibilities, she can now take three extended vacations per year (without her phone!) while still knowing her business will move forward when she is gone.

3. Identify and overcome your blind spots.

Often, business leaders come to Entre Results because they are seeking help in a specific area of the business. After going through a comprehensive onboarding process, we usually clearly identify the top few areas that will substantially help the business to thrive. As we begin to assess the needs of the business, we also assess the communication and leadership style of the business owners and other key leaders involved in the organization. There are many research-based personality tests available to help us understand leaders (I recommend the DISC profile as one of the possible assessments). Through these assessments, along with simple observation and interacting with the business leadership team, the coaches at Entre Results begin to identify blind spots and put together a game plan to overcome the ignored problems.

At one point, we were contacted by Lewis, the owner of a larger than normal plumbing company, who had seen one of our videos and connected with the message. He mentioned that business had been steadily growing over the last three years, but recently the business had taken a downturn. Two of the younger, but very effective employees in the company had recently quit to go work for a competitor. Lewis wanted to keep talented people like these employees who had left, so he was seeking coaching for his four key leaders, but not for himself. We approached Lewis's situation with these steps:

1. An Entre Results coach met with the four leaders but was also adamant about meeting with Lewis, at least for the first three months of the coaching process. Lewis reluctantly agreed.

2. Everyone going through the coaching process underwent several different assessments, including a DISC assessment.

3. We also had one of the key leaders reach out to one of the employees who had left and ask the employee to answer a few questions for a very simple exit interview.

The coach soon discovered that Lewis had been going through some major personal problems and some days would get into negative moods. During those days, everyone avoided him like the plague. He completely killed the morale of everyone around him. It wasn't that he would yell at his employees, but he would cause a tension around the office that was unbearable.

Once our coach had collected all of this information, he told Lewis what was going on and that Lewis was the main reason why the two key employees had left. Nobody else had mustered the courage to tell Lewis directly what was going on, but everyone knew he was the problem. Upon receiving the news, Lewis wasn't too happy—it wasn't a positive coaching session in his mind. From our perspective, however, it was good and necessary to have that conversation. After two days of thinking the situation over, Lewis called his coach and apologized for not taking the news well.

He agreed to more long-term coaching, and although he committed to working on his blind spots, it took him many months to really commit to change. He finally began to empower his employees to give more direct feedback to him, and he also sought personal counseling for the other areas of his personal life that were struggling. A year later, the culture and environment were transformed.

4. Find out what motivates your employees and use it to manage them.

The harsh reality of the workforce is that few employees are truly motivated to perform at a high level at their job every day.

In fact, it's difficult even for owners to operate at a consistently high level. The first step to keeping employees inspired is for the leader to understand their own motivational styles and how they are currently motivating their staff. Usually, there are two or three styles leaders are favoring, and often one is the most dominant.

During one of our speaking engagements, we were introduced to Brent, an owner of a consulting company in the oil and gas industry. He was frustrated because no matter how hard he tried, he was not able to keep his staff engaged and motivated to perform at a high level. When he chose to engage a coach on our team and we began to assess his business, we were initially pleasantly surprised. His organization had an effective hiring process compared to others we had seen. They were missing a few tools that would have helped identify motivation before bringing the employee into the company, but besides that they were in good shape. Additionally, employees had a good grasp of the core values and the purpose of the company. The reason I mention those two areas is that core values and a thorough, intentional hiring process significantly affect a company's ability to maintain a motivated staff.

We soon discovered Brent was highly motivated by financial reward. In fact, financial reward was his dominant motivational style that trumped all other styles. Therefore, he was constantly challenging his team to win by giving them bonuses for results, as well as paying them higher salaries than most other companies. During the coaching process, however, he soon realized that money was the only way he was motivating people. In reality, it was a selfish way to motivate employees because he was discounting all of the other motivational styles. In fact, there are eight ways to motivate team members:

1. Sense of Belonging.

A positive community can be incredibly powerful when it comes to motivating employees. Most people have an innate desire to belong, especially if there are perceptible benefits to being a part of the group.

2. Public Recognition.

Many of us crave recognition and affirmation. We love being celebrated, cheered, and respected. And to have it all happen in front of a group of people? Even better! Sales divisions often motivate their employees through public recognition because it complements extroverted personalities.

3. Private Recognition

Not everyone is motivated by public recognition. Some people may be anxious about having to stand out from the crowd, and others may feel uncomfortable with all the attention. For those individuals, private recognition is usually much more effective. Remembering and recognizing employees' birthdays, anniversaries, and other milestones is crucial and has the bonus effect of strengthening the sense of belonging in your workplace.

4. Monetary Reward

Probably the most tried and true of all motivating strategies is monetary reward. It's straightforward, easy to implement (especially when business is going well), and it speaks to something many of us have with us at all times—our wallets! When using this method of motivation, it is important to have a clear, fair structure in place. Employees must know how they can earn their monetary reward up front so that they have something to work toward.

5. Fear of Consequences

Motivating through fear of consequences is probably the one that makes most people uncomfortable. Although it may sound harsh to some, consequences really are necessary in order to motivate some employees. They might be motivated by the fear of missing out on recognition or monetary reward. Or they may fear letting the group down. Regardless of the source of the fear, savvy managers can use it to create clear boundaries of appropriate work behavior and effort.

One thing to be aware of with this motivating technique is the importance of having fair and clear consequences. Employees need to know what the boundaries are and what consequences can be expected. They also need to see consistent application of rules and boundaries so that they know consequences are not driven by emotion. Any consequences should also be carefully considered so that they are fair and proportional to the rule, guideline, or boundary. Fear of consequences must be balanced with other positive workplace motivations in order to truly be effective.

6. Competition

Competitions are a common, and powerful, motivating tool in the workplace. Some people simply need to compete in order to achieve their best work and productivity. Think of company competitions in the same dynamic as a healthy, effective sports team who thrives on competition, working hard and striving to improve themselves so that they can achieve results.

They aim to be the best individual players they can be, but as a unit are still working toward the common goals of the team. In order for competitions to truly be effective, they need to be implemented in a way that encourages your workforce.

Keep in mind that competition should be friendly and have clear ground rules and consequences for not playing fair. A competition that pits employees against each other can quickly dismantle and divide your working environment. Usually, unhealthy competition happens when people don't align with the core values of the company and do not view integrity the same. However, as long as you've trained your employees about the company's guiding principles, a well-implemented competition will develop a sense of urgency for everyone in your business and can be a fun way to create a new energy.

7. Significance/Purpose

Much has been written about the changing motivations of young people entering the workforce—specifically millennials. Research shows that many of these young people are no longer motivated by pay increases and stock options. Instead, they want to know how a business intends to contribute to society. Many people just beginning their careers want to know that their daily work matters for more than just a biweekly paycheck. They want to know how their efforts fit into the bigger picture and that their hard work is contributing to something larger than themselves. As we become a more collaborative society, thanks to improved communication and connections (the Internet, smartphones, social media, etc.), many people desire that their efforts are not selfish or purely driven by capitalism. For these individuals, it is important that you have a clear company mission and purpose. They will work even harder when they can believe in the work that you're doing. In order to motivate using significance and purpose, it is also necessary for you as a leader to understand the value systems of your varied employees.

8. Life Balance

Life balance can be an excellent motivational tool for employees. If they see that their work allows them the balance to live into their passions, they will be motivated to work hard during the time they're in office. Some small business owners may even allow their employees to telecommute or work from home. By offering proof that life balance is valued, you can often instill loyalty and trust in employees. They will respond with hard work and appreciation.

As a result of going through the coaching sessions, Brent gave his team several assessments to learn how they were best motivated. Even once he determined motivational styles, he needed to start implementing, though it was initially hard for him to change his own preferences. But he continued to work at it and over the months began to see improvements among his employees. What surprised him was the varying degrees in which his employees responded. Some made reasonable progress, but one person exhibited a complete 180-degree change. This employee had been struggling, slacking, and was in danger of being let go, but when motivated according to his personality, he became one of the top performers in the company. Brent continued to implement varied motivational styles and was happy to see more consistent motivation and work ethic among his employees throughout the months.

5. Write down your plan because structure fulfills purpose.

When many people start a business, they are told to create a business plan. Often, first-time business owners don't know where to start, so they usually grab some type of template and haphazardly put something together. Or, if they are trying to raise capital, they will put together an elaborate plan or even hire somebody to help them create this plan. It often looks beautiful on paper, stocked with graphs and charts, and it's important to actually go through the process of creating a plan at the beginning because it does force you to think about areas you normally wouldn't think about. The problem is that once complete, the business plan is never looked at again. It's a dead document, instead of a living document. The even bigger crime is that since leaders never used the original plan, as the business grows, the leadership team often doesn't believe in developing a new plan because they never looked at their original business plan. To them, it seems like a waste of time.

This situation is very similar to when we first met Stephanie, the owner of a very small social media marketing company. While she had an old plan, she never looked at it and hesitated to create anything new. She had a lot of clarity over where she wanted to go with the business and knew she was growing fast, so she was willing to give coaching a try, although she was still a bit guarded with her expectations.

After meeting with Stephanie and discussing her goals, we implemented the following:

1. We took a look at her old plan and pulled about five percent of the ideas that were still applicable to her business.

2. We began to work with Stephanie and one other person in her company to create a much simpler

plan. However, we not only created the goals, but we also got very detailed over the activities that would reach those goals.

3. Her company didn't have a marketing plan, even though they had helped many of their clients create their own marketing plans. We created a plan with them.

4. We noticed that Stephanie's company did awesome work for their clients on social media, but they were not implementing those strategies on their own business. We helped them simply do for themselves what they did for their clients.

5. We established regular meetings or accountability sessions to make sure that they were looking at and following the plan.

The result was that Stephanie landed some top 40 under 40 awards in her community, and her small social media company began to grow into a still small but mighty company. When they began to grow, they spent less time looking at their plan and even began decreasing their regular meetings. The business began to falter. So, they went back to looking at the plan, following structure, and the company began to thrive again.

6. Know your numbers, inside and out.

With the exception of business owners who have a financial background, the leaders of almost all young companies rarely look at their financial statements. Many individuals look at the Profit and Loss Statement, Balance Sheet, and Cash Flow Statement like they are trying to read ancient Greek. Also, many people love the results of making money but hate analyzing the numbers to make sure money is being made. Usually, they just try to sell more and hope for the best in creating cash. I could personally relate to this typical individual before I really started to see the absolute necessity of learning the language of business, which involves knowing the numbers inside out.

One of our coaches at Entre Results met Howard, a business owner in the commercial cleaning business, at a local networking event. Howard wanted some sales coaching to help take his company to the next level. He was fascinated with sales, loved generating more revenue, and wanted to keep pumping up that top line. After going through a business strategy session, one of our coaches quickly pointed out that Howard's business was in a very dangerous situation financially. Howard didn't understand, so the coach chose to invest a good portion of their coaching sessions toward explaining the financial numbers to Howard before they began sales coaching.

They worked on a few items:

1. They realized that one of their offerings wasn't making any money at all. They would actually lose money if they sold that specific service.

2. A few packages were created that provided higher margins and ultimately helped generate more cash.

3. Howard realized that the crews were not staffed appropriately. They easily decreased that cost by providing less hours to two of the part-time employees.

4. Howard hadn't included his salary in the profit and loss statement, so it wasn't an accurate picture. They made the change.

5. They put together a plan to create a business emergency fund. It would protect the business when it had a bad month or two, so they would

not need to rely on the bank to help with cash flow during tough times.

Working on the numbers with Howard initially made his life much more stressful. He began to see things for the way they truly were in his business. It hurts knowing the truth. However, once he made it to the other side and the numbers started looking better, he actually reduced his stress. The emergency fund took off pressure, and he could focus on selling more in a much less stressful environment.

7. Project what your life will look like in three years

At the very heart and core of our business coaching model, we believe businesses should be created to give owners the life they want for themselves. Why should people undergo the risk of starting a business if there is not great reward? But in the midst of growing a business, that original dream of the owner is sometimes lost. Because that goal is easy to lose sight of, we love asking business leaders, "What do you want your life to look like in three years?" Answering this question is such a great reminder to stay focused, and it helps you create a business model that can work toward that personal goal. The three-year number is far enough in the future to allow your dreams to be achieved, but not too far away that it seems too distant.

One of our coaches first met Ron, the owner of a computer repair company, at a local restaurant. They were both waiting for their parties to arrive and began to strike up a conversation. Ron eventually struck up a business coaching relationship, and one of the first questions our coach asked Ron was, "What do you want your life to look like in three years?" As it turned out, Ron wanted to create a business that would run and operate with only one virtual meeting per week. He wanted to be able to take off and work with an orphanage in Honduras for two years. His goal was to simply talk every week on the phone with his manager and come home every quarter to check up on things for one week.

The Entre Results coach took Ron through our entire coaching process. Ron was coachable and willing to take risks to achieve his vision. His coach took him through a process to build in incremental change.

1. Ron was very busy, so his coach first began to figure out how to free up Ron's time, deciding to have Ron hire a full-time personal assistant. The assistant took over scheduling, admin, and any tasks that Ron could teach to the assistant and delegate.

2. Ron and his coach determined who would be ideal clients for the business and began to heavily focus on the clients Ron could most serve. They also looked at how to target higher-end clients and how to create a quality experience for them. Ron also began to let go of the clients who were headaches and were generating less revenue.

3. The next step was to clean up Ron's books and make sure his financial statements were in very clear order. The short-term result of this work was that they realized Ron's overhead was too high and he could move his business to a smaller space without any negative effect on the business. The long-term result was that Ron would easily be able to check in on his company's financial status while he was away.

4. Ron began to clearly articulate the values of the company to his employees, discussing them in meetings and placing visual reminders around the office for everyone to see throughout the day.

5. Everyone on Ron's team was given assessments. Some people's roles were tweaked in order to

maximize skill sets and productivity, and Ron also hired another person who would be able to fill in the gaps once Ron was gone.

6. Ron began to do test runs away from the office, taking off two weeks at a time to see how the company functioned.

7. Ron's coach worked with him to put away an entire year of operating expenses, paying off all of the company debt and reducing risks caused by any future setbacks.

It was a constant march forward, with occasional steps backwards. Ron's goal wasn't easy, but after three years of hard and smart work, Ron jumped on a plane to Honduras and began the next season of his life. He also gave every employee the opportunity to come and serve with him for one week. Ron still conducted one-hour weekly staff meetings via video conferencing, reviewed monthly financial statements, and traveled back every quarter to check in with the business. However, besides that, he lived in Honduras and fulfilled his dream.

How does your business measure up to these seven principles? Have you pinpointed areas you know will help improve your business? Now that you have considered the principles, resolve to improve the areas you know you are weak in. Determine what resources you need to cultivate or what action steps you need to implement in order to bring about change.

At Entre Results, we want you to be able to create a business that gives you the life you want to live. We also want to empower you to in turn give your employees the life they want to live, and to create a business that blesses your family and enriches your community. It is our goal to give our clients the platform to serve their community, country, and world.

These goals are not possible, however, unless you commit to change and take control of your business and of your life.

If you would like to have a conversation about how our coaching team can support you, contact us at EntreResults. com. We would love to partner with you as you become a better leader and work to grow your business.

Entre Results

---

tre Results offers a wide variety of coaching packages customized to fit
ur needs as an executive, salesperson, or business owner and tailored to
u and your goals.

ENTRE RESULTS EXECUTIVE DEVELOPMENT
Ideal for a leadership team of three to ten people, this package equips
participants to find their stride, become better leaders, and grow their
business or department effectively.

ENTRE RESULTS SALES PERFORMANCE
This service supports sales teams and individual salesmen who want to
strengthen their sales prowess and all-around sales performance, building
in accountability both with coaches and with peers to help sales
professionals reach their sales goals.

ENTRE RESULTS OWNER EXCELLENCE
The best option for business owners or those with stakes in small
businesses, in this service we will analyze your business based on the
seven key areas of business and strengthen each area to help you build a
functional, innovative business that achieves your goals.

ENTRE BALANCE LIFE IMPROVEMENT
If you feel out of balance or are simply unable to move forward in your life,
this is the coaching package for you. It covers every aspect of your life,
helping you grow as an individual and reach your goals in your
professional and personal life.

ENTRE RESULTS INDIVIDUAL ACCOMPLISHMENT
This package's goal is to help individuals achieve their business goals and
is designed for solopreneurs, sales individuals, direct sales teams, and
other one to two person groups.

or more information about these packages or to
start achieving your goals, contact us today!

WWW.ENTRERESULTS.COM

CONGRATULATIONS ON COMPLETING THE JOURNEY OF ENTREBUSINESS!

READY TO GET STARTED WITH THE NEXT STEPS TO GROWING YOUR BUSINESS?

CHECK OUT THE LINK BELOW TO DOWNLOAD OUR FREE RESOURCE, "SMALL BUSINESS PLANNING"!

ENTRERESULTS.COM/ENTREBUSINESS

CPSIA information can be obtained
at www.ICGtesting.com
Printed in the USA
FFOW04n0516231216
30366FF